Developing Early Maths through Story

Step-by-step advice for using storytelling as a springboard for maths activities

By Marion Leeper

Published by Practical Pre-School Books, A Division of MA Education Ltd, St Jude's Church, Dulwich Road, Herne Hill, London, SE24 0PB.

Tel: 020 7738 5454 www.practicalpreschoolbooks.com

© MA Education Ltd 2015

Design: Alison Coombes **fonthill**creative 01722 717043

All images © MA Education Ltd. All photos taken by Marion Leeper, with the exceptio[...] [...]arlier.
Back cover image of Marion Leeper © Derek Langley (www.darknessandlight.co.uk).

ISBN 978-1-909280-76-2

Introduction

Who this book is for

Francis, playing with a handful of pegs and a wooden board, was shouting at the top of his voice. *'I can't help it!'*, he told me, *'Maths is so exciting!'*

This book is for any adult working with children – educator, care-giver, childminder, or teacher – who would like to find that excitement in the rich world of mathematics, and explore the mathematical possibilities in their everyday activities with children.

Mathematics and story

Traditional stories are full of numbers: three wishes, seven brothers, twelve princesses...

Numbers help to set up the pattern of the story: the first two pigs came to grief, but what about the third one? Children – and adults – use **stories to help them make sense of the world**: stories give us words and images which help us express our feelings.

Mathematics, too, is a way of **ordering experience**: taking objects and events in the real world and working out connections between them.

The patterns of mathematics and the patterns of storytelling often overlap. I told the story of 'Teremok', (page 7) in which animals crowd into a tiny house. The next day I found Adam, age 3, barring the door of the playhouse, calling out: *'You can't come in'*. Why don't you say: "Come and live with us," I suggested, in the words of the story. Suddenly his whole attitude changed as he tried to see how many children he could fit in the house. His mathematical learning involved a whole lot of social and emotional learning too.

For adults, tuning into the emotional potential of sharing a plate of cakes, for instance, makes teaching mathematics easier: it becomes not just a dry set of logical rules but a **vital life skill**.

How to use this book

Using story as a way into mathematics can be empowering for adults and children alike and can take away some of the anxiety sometimes associated with mathematics. These **stories will embody abstract mathematical concepts**, making them easier for children to understand. The stories are interactive, leaving space in the story for children to respond and to join in, allowing them to explore ideas in their own way, and to take their learning off in new directions.

Each chapter starts with a story connected to a particular set of **learning objectives**. It shows how mathematical talk can be built into the story and suggests open-ended activities to follow up. To encourage rich talk and purposeful play, I've suggested real world objects and outdoor activities. The activities are aimed at children age 3-5, but each chapter includes suggestions of what mathematics might look like for younger children and babies.

Watching children make mathematical discoveries is deeply rewarding. As they tackle even the simplest operation, they access many different skills, making connections with what they already know. Even the mistakes they make give us an insight into what skilled learners they are. Each chapter gives examples of what children do and say, and suggests ways of capturing these 'footprints in the sand' – the fleeting glimpses of learning.

It is hoped that this book will encourage you to think of new and wonderful ways into the world of mathematics; and persuade you that mathematics is a powerful way for young children to explore their world.

Tips on telling stories

The traditional folktales in this book are intended to be told, not read. Although links are included where possible to appropriate picturebook versions, **telling the story** has many advantages:

- It allows you to get closer to the children, to make eye contact with them and notice how they respond.

- It encourages children to become involved, for instance by inviting them to join in with the text or the actions; by using their ideas.

- It models ways that children can make their own stories.

However, telling a story without a book is easier than it sounds. **You are already a storyteller if you have ever:**

- Stopped reading the words of a book to talk about the pictures.

- Changed the text, for instance, to make it longer or shorter.

- Told children something interesting that once happened to you.

- Simply played about with a story in any way.

A few strategies will make storytelling easy and fun:

- Start within your comfort zone, with a personal story or a familiar text. Keep the book near you just in case.

- Take a little time to plan the story. Divide it into three or four sections, and make a mental picture as a 'signpost' to each section. Work out your first and last sentence and you're away!

- Act larger than life when you tell a story. Start with a smile and a commanding voice. Exaggerate your gestures, your tone of voice – don't be afraid to clown around.

- Invite the children to take part: suggesting ideas, joining in with the words, or making sound effects.

- Respond to the children's cues. If they are getting restless, move on quickly: if they are interested, follow their suggestions, preferably without losing the thread of the story.

- If you can, listen to professional storytellers.

- Tell lots of stories! The more you do, the easier it gets.

How to use this book

EYFS Maths Objectives

The **learning objectives** for each chapter offer children a wide and rich experience across the **EYFS Maths curriculum**. However, when children are allowed to explore freely, their learning may take off in many different directions. As practitioners we need to trust children as learners and understand that they will revisit these concepts in their own good time.

Resources

Where possible these props are **real world objects**, non-plastic, to encourage richer language and more holistic exploration. Offering children high quality resources and trusting them (under supervision) with precious objects makes them feel respected. Other suggestions include easily-found, everyday props that can be left for children to play with freely.

For many stories you can use a story mat to put props on. It's easy to make a story mat of your own, using a green cloth for grass, a blue one for water, and scraps of fabric for other landscape features. Alternatively use different-shaped cloths that you can unfold gradually (see page 28).

Once upon a number

Each story is linked to a number. Particular numbers have importance for different children ('3! that's my number! I'm 3'), but they also lend themselves to different areas of mathematics.

Why this story?

This section describes how the story fits well with an area of mathematics and which parts of the story may be especially appropriate for children with particular interests or schemas. It also describes the emotional affordances of the story: why it's an engaging story for children.

Story outline

The story can be read, but it is intended to be retold, adapting where necessary to suit a particular group.

It includes a brief 'Story summary', for ease of remembering (as below).

Anansi asks Rabbit to share his five cakes; but Rabbit only gives him one.	Anansi keeps scaring Rabbit away: each time he steals one more cake.	Rabbit swaps the plates, so he gets all the cakes back and Anansi has none.

Joining in with the story

The 'Joining in' section expands on the storytelling advice on page 3. When children become **involved in the story**, they are more likely to remember it, to retell their own versions, and to share their mathematical thinking.

Big questions

These are 'Big questions' because they address issues that are important to children. If children are given an opportunity to talk, they may raise some of these questions themselves. Others can form starting points for follow-up investigations, or for the children's own stories. There are questions about empathy and emotions, as well as mathematical questions. There are questions designed **to encourage children to engage in mathematics for a reason** – so rather than asking a question to which the adult already knows the answer ('How many pine cones?'), they encourage children to count as a way of solving a problem ('Do we have enough cakes for everyone?' 'Do you think we have more than ten?'). They include open-ended questions to which there is no wrong answer. There are also closed questions with only one possible answer: but here too it is important to value all the children's answers. Wrong answers are to be treasured, as a useful as a way into discussion: *'Well done, you counted the dinosaurs. You said 3, when Charlie said 4: how could that have happened? Which do you think it really is? How could we check?'*.

Example stories

Telling a story often creates another story. **Children's responses to mathematics**, in their own stories and their play, is at the core of this book. In children's play, it may not be obvious at first where the mathematics is. It's tempting to break in with inappropriate mathematical questions: 'So how many conkers have you got?' or 'Can you just add those cakes together for me?', instead of listening and reflecting on the children's meaning. Some of the children's own stories in this book don't appear to have relevant maths in them: that's fine. The mathematical concept may emerge much later in a different context. But while the children are playing with the props, the maths is sinking in.

Follow-up activities

Many of these activities are adult-led, but almost all of them should be followed up (or preceded) by free exploration of the materials: this is the time to assess children's understanding and engage in their mathematical thinking.

Circle games

Games for a group of children led by an adult, including rhymes and turn-taking games. Some of them could be adapted by children to play on their own.

Daily routines

Mathematics is all around us! This section contains suggestions for recognising the mathematics we incorporate into our daily life without thinking about it, whether cooking, eating, or tidying up.

Outdoor activities

Some children learn better on their feet. These activities use natural materials, the outdoor environment, or space for active and energetic games.

Using ICT

The suggestions for ICT applications are based on current technology available. For the pros and cons of children using ICT, visit the BBC website article (www.bbc.co.uk/guides/z3tsyrd). **Make sure ICT use is safe, supervised at all times and any websites are checked before use with children.**

Younger children

This section highlights a few everyday activities that babies and toddlers love to do and shows how favourite games can lay the foundations of future mathematical thinking.

Footprints in the sand: mark-making & assessment

This section suggests what to look for and where to look when **assessing children's learning**, as well as ways of encouraging children to record their mathematics, either by making marks on paper, or by making arrangements, models or pictures.

Songs and additional stories

Beginning with a song is a great way for children to make their voice heard in a safe context before they are asked to volunteer ideas and answers. Some of the songs are maths-related, others just fit the subject of the story. For educators who feel anxious about oral stories, or who want to extend the topic, there are suggestions of picture books that support the same area of mathematics.

Links to other parts of the book

Some stories are a good way into more than one area of mathematics. Links to these 'extra' bits of maths are suggested at the end of each chapter.

Number Zero — Empty

EYFS Maths Objectives

✓ Know that things exist, even when out of sight (Number 16-20 mths).

✓ Separate a group of three or four objects in different ways, beginning to recognise that the total is still the same (Number 30-50 mths).

Resources

A box with a lid, a toy mouse and other woodland animals, a woodland role play scene made with a pile of leaves and other natural objects arranged on a piece of fabric.

Teremok, or The Little House in the Forest

This traditional folktale from Russia, about animals sharing a house, explores different ways of dividing up a group of objects; the concepts of none, more and gone; and feelings about friends and sharing.

Once upon a number: zero

Zero plays the same part in the dance of numbers that silence plays in a piece of music. Although it's a mathematically difficult concept, children like the idea of a number that represents nothing at all: when children have guessed a million exciting things that might be inside, the sight of an empty box is an enchanting surprise.

Why this story?

For babies, noticing that something has gone is the beginning of learning about number. When they realise that the mouse is still in the box, even when the lid is on, they also understand that their mother can be out of the room, but will still come

Story outline: Jeremok, or The Little House in the Forest

Mousie Brown was running through the forest looking for a new home. She found a box. *'I wonder who lives here?'* she said.

'Tere-tere-mok,

Who will answer when I knock?'

No answer! There was nobody in the box.

'Just right for me,' said Mousie Brown and climbed in the box. She hadn't been there long when mole shuffled past. He knocked on the box:

'Tere-tere-mok,

Who will answer when I knock?'

'It's Mousie Brown. Come and live with me,'

They hadn't been there long when the squirrel came jumping past. She knocked on the box:

'Tere-tere-mok,

Who will answer when I knock?'

It's Mousie Brown and mole. Come and live with us.'

They hadn't been there long when the frog hopped past. He knocked on the box:

'Tere-tere-mok,

Who will answer when I knock?'

'It's Mousie Brown, mole and squirrel. Come and live with us.'

Then clumsy brown bear came stamping past. He knocked on the box with his big bear claws and called out in a big bear voice:

'Tere-tere-mok,

Who will answer when I knock?'

'It's Mousie Brown, mole, squirrel and frog. You can't live with us: you're too big.'

'Then I'll just sit on top,' said the brown bear. Out jumped Mousie Brown, mole, squirrel and frog and ran back to their own homes, just in time, before the bear sat on the box and squashed it flat.

Story summary

Mousie Brown and her 3 friends live in the woods. Mousie Brown finds an empty box to live in.	One by one, her friends come and join her in the box. There's just room for all of them.	The big bear can't fit in the box, so he sits on top and squashes it.

back – an important step towards independence as well as mathematical awareness.

For older children, 'zero' plays an important but invisible part in the story: as the animals meet and make friends in the box, they have to leave their real homes empty. In this story, re-arranging toys together and apart, and finding out all the different ways of making four, is also a way of thinking about friendship and joining groups. Children with containing schemas, who like wrapping things up and putting them in boxes, enjoy this story.

Joining in with the story

The children can help arrange the woodland scene, establishing that there is one animal in each place: one mole in a hole, one squirrel in a bush, one frog on a log, one mouse in the grass. They can use the props to help re-enact the story, choosing which animal will knock on the box next, and remembering who is already in the box. (You can also use the names of the children for the characters: Rumi the squirrel, Charlotte the mole.)

The children can knock on the floor in time to the words, getting the rhythm of the language in their bodies, an important skill for learning to count. A repetitive story like this makes it easy for children to join in with the words. And of course, there are many opportunities for children to count how many animals inside the box, how many outside, and to work out that there are always four animals. But even if numbers are not mentioned, a lot of mathematical thinking is still going on.

Big questions

- Can you see all the animals? How many are there altogether? How else could we arrange them?

- What do you think is in the box? How many animals in the box? How many animals outside the box? Are there still 4?

- Now another animal is in the box, are there the same number as last time? Are there always going to be 4? How do you know that?

- What's the best number of animals to have in the box? How does the mouse feel when there are lots of animals in the box?

- Can you show me bear claws? A bear voice? Should we let the bear in the box? Why not? How does the bear feel? When do you like to be with your friends? When do you like to be on your own?

- Can you remember where the animals' proper homes are?

Example stories from children

Daisy's story used props from the Teremok story. It may not have any numbers in it, but the mathematical thinking is still there!

Daisy's story

The animals are eating some grass. The cow's looking in the volcano to see if there's any food. But there isn't any in there. The snake keeps getting in the farm to eat the butterflies. He wants Daisy to eat the butterflies but Daisy won't. He's going in the box!

'Have you seen my friend Mr. Snake?' says the frog. 'Is he in the box? Oh yes he is!' He's got out. 'You're good at eating butterflies Mr. Snake.'

Chloe and Liam's game started when James put Mousie Brown in the box and covered him with a leaf. Their story explored the idea of full and empty, piling all the animals in the box, and then piling them up elsewhere. They also resolve their own sharing issues, as successfully as the animals in the original story.

Liam and Chloe's story

Liam: Mousie brown's in the box.
Chloe: I think he's sleepy.
Liam: He's got a leaf on top.
Chloe: Maybe it's a blanket...
Liam: I found something different: a coconut! (picks up pine cone) (Chloe takes all the animals out of the box)
Liam: There's nobody in the box!

Chloe: They're over here! They're having a nap.
Liam: Here's Mousie brown.
Chloe: He's mine.
Liam: He's mine...There you go (gives Chloe mouse)
Chloe: Let's put them in the box. They're getting cold! They're getting cold!
Liam: Quick! Put the lid on?
Chloe: Who's going to put the lid on? (James puts it on) Thank you James.

Follow-up activities

Using the props: when the animals are safely back home, we can count them to make sure there are 4 altogether. Then children can make their own scenarios, choosing different ways of arranging the animals, with an adult modelling mathematical language: 'One in the leaves, one in the grass, and two in the box, that's four.'

Introducing 'number stories': explain that numbers can tell stories as well as words: the story 'there was a mole, a squirrel and a mouse in the box, a frog on a log' can be replaced by numbers: three here, one there: four all together. Include number zero: 'Four in the box and zero outside.' Introduce mathematical words carefully – plus, add, equals, makes, and ask the children to repeat them with you, explain what they mean and then use them in context. Children love to learn technical language – though they may not remember the words straight away.

More stories: the same props can be used for many different scenarios which will lend themselves to number stories. What if:

- The animals are playing hide and seek. Where are they going to hide? Together or apart? Who is going to find them?

- The animals are all playing together. $(4 + 0 = 4)$. They have a quarrel, and each go off on their own. $(1 + 1 + 1 + 1 = 4)$. How are they going to make friends again? What will they say to each other?

- One animal wants to shift a heavy log on their own, but it is too heavy. How will they ask for help? How many animals will they need?

More role-play ideas: children may not tell stories in response to yours immediately. Don't panic! It takes a while for them to internalise the learning and to move on to a new game. They may use a completely different role-play scenario. What about:

- A garage or train depot with one more car than parking spaces.

- A small world farm with four different fields.

- A collection of large real leaves and model minibeasts.

Circle games

- **Play I-spy:** ask the children to arrange the animals for you, then suggest things to spy: 'I spy 2 animals in the long grass.' 'I spy an animal with green skin in the pond…'. Can the children name the animals you are thinking of?

Daily routines

- When getting a group of children together for a snack or story, give them instructions about where you want them to sit. '2 on the cushion, 1 on the chair, 1 on the mat.' Then keep changing your mind. '3 on the mat, 1 on the cushion, nobody on the chair.' Ask the children for their suggestions.

Outdoor play

- **Provide a collection of large boxes:** how many children can fit in each one? Re-enact the story with children in a large box.

- **Go on an egg box treasure hunt:** give the children each an egg box and invite them to put one treasure (a leaf, feather, or pebble, for instance) in each section. Then provide a tray with only four compartments for them to sort their egg box treasure into.

Using ICT

- Invite children to rearrange, hide, and count animals in a forest, jungle or zoo, using, for example, the 'Tiny Hearts' app Pocket Zoo (http://tinyhearts.com/pocketzoo).

- Train a webcam in the garden area and encourage children to monitor how many people there are. How many on the bikes, and how many in the sand? Is your friend outside? Is there space for you?

Younger children

- **Play with a cloth:** covering babies up with a cloth and whisking it off again often gets a really good giggle as you teach them that you can make the whole world disappear and it will come back again.

- **Play with leaves:** dropping them, shaking leaves on a cloth so they fly about, hiding toys underneath the leaves and finding them again.

- **Find more places to hide and find toys** – in boxes, in bubbles in the bath, or in sand, or under cushions and rugs.

- **Use pop-up toys on sticks:** make the toy 'disappear' and then make it pop up again.

- **Play with food** – arranging it different ways on a plate. '1 piece of bread under the potato, 1 piece on top of the tomato…'.

Footprints in the sand

Mark-making

- Tell the children you are having trouble remembering where all the animals are. Use a large leaf and a black pen to write the numbers of animals in each place. For example, I asked Chloe to help me decide what to write: *'There's a mouse in the box, write mouse. And there's a… a hedgehog! Write hedgehog. And look! I've found a squirrel. Write squirrel. It's 's', it's long and wriggly.'* Shane watched what I was doing and said *'Can I have a pen?'* He looked for the biggest leaf he could find, and then spent a long time making marks all over it.

- Provide paper or a simple map of the small world setup so that the children can record where the creatures are hiding. Invite them to retell their story in a picture or a home made book.

- Once children have experimented with their own ways of recording numbers, they will begin to understand the purpose of written mathematics. At this point it is appropriate to introduce wooden numerals and show them conventional

Mousie Brown
Up the tall white candlestick
Went little mousie brown.
Right to the top and she couldn't get down.
So she called for her grandma: 'Grandma!'
But Grandma was in town.
So she curled into a little ball
And rolled herself back down.

(Source: traditional, Matteson, E. *This Little Puffin*)

This well-known rhyme is still one of the best ways for babies to explore the idea of 'here' and 'gone' especially with finger-puppet birds as props.

Two little dicky birds
Two little dickie birds sat on the wall
One called Peter, one called Paul.
Fly away Peter, fly away Paul
Come back Peter, come back Paul

(Source: traditional, Matteson, E. *This Little Puffin*)

Additional stories

- Text of the story at: russian-crafts.com/russian-folk-tales/teremok-little-hut.html

- Adams, P. *Old Macdonald had a Farm*

- Dodd, L. and Sutton, E. *My Cat Likes to Hide in Boxes*

- Donaldson, J. A *Squash and a Squeeze*

- Lupton, H. *Freaky Tales from Far and Wide* (contains another version of this story, the House in the Skull)

- Rosen, M. and Graham, B. *This is our House*

ways of recording numbers. Allow the children to arrange the animals on the mat and tell their own story: 'there are 2 in the box, 1 in the tree and 1 in the river'. Then use the wooden numbers to record the number story: 1 + 1 + 2 = 4.

Assessment opportunities

- Take pictures of the children's arrangements of animals, and record the language they use to describe how the animals are grouped.

- Listen out for mathematical language children use spontaneously in their stories: do they show that they can arrange a group of animals different ways? Do they talk about what they are doing?

- Notice when children spontaneously help out with everyday problems arranging small groups of objects.

What to look for

Can children count up to four animals accurately? Can they think of new ways to divide up a group of animals? Do they use words like: more, less, plus, makes, zero, none, gone?

Songs

This song makes a great beginning to the story, you can add in more verses, suggesting different family members who might come and help.

Links to other parts of the book

This module fits well with:

✓ Number 3: position and direction

✓ Number 5: counting arrangements of objects

✓ Number 13: size and boxes

Number One – Counting

EYFS Maths Objectives

✔ Notice changes in the number of objects (Number birth-11 mths).

✔ Know that a group of things changes in quantity when something is added or taken away (Number 22-36 mths).

✔ Say the number that is one more than a given number (Number 40-60 mths).

✔ Find one more or one less from a group of up to five objects, then ten objects (Number 40-60 mths).

Anansi's Tea Party

Based on the adventures of Anansi the spider, the Caribbean trickster who likes to get something for nothing, the story explores the related mathematical concepts of adding one, taking one away, and sharing.

Resources

Two plates, two puppets, and five pretend cakes: model food, real cakes, or cakes made with the children from dough or clay.

Once upon a number: 1

One is a puzzling number to mathematicians and a powerful one for children: it helps them make the big step in understanding that counting is the same as adding on one each time. At about the same time they often gain the physical dexterity to point to one object at a time – it's all part of learning to count accurately, with one-to-one correspondence.

Why this story?

This is a story for children who love transporting objects, as they move cakes from one plate to the other.

number. One will undo the work of another. This is such an obvious concept to adults that we can't remember learning it: but it's a vital building block in the development of mathematics.

When it's a question of how much cake, children have a fine sense of what's fair: they know when someone has one more than them, or when they have less. As Anansi steals the cakes one at a time, and Rabbit tries to work out what's wrong, the children are encouraged to talk about important questions of sharing and justice. The story shows how mathematics can help make life fairer.

Joining in with the story

This is the pantomime of maths stories. Children enjoy the drama as naughty Anansi steals the cakes. They love calling out to Rabbit when he comes out of hiding, telling him what Anansi has done, while Anansi tries to stop them.

You can count the cakes several times at the beginning of the story, to establish there are definitely five. An odd number of cakes makes the problems of sharing more interesting.

The children can take turns being sneaky Anansi and stealing a cake from the plate, or predicting in advance what will happen each time he steals a cake. When Rabbit comes

It gives children practical experience of what happens if you add one more object to a set, and shows them how adding and subtracting are linked together. Put one more cake on a plate, then take it away, and you'll end up with the same

Story outline: Anansi's Tea Party

Rabbit was busy cooking. He had made five delicious cakes. There was a knock on the door: Anansi the spider. Anansi is always hungry and he likes to play tricks.

'Rabbit, those cakes smell so good!' said Anansi. *'Will you share them with me?'*

'All right, Anansi, you can have one.' Rabbit put one cake on a plate for Anansi. Now Rabbit had four cakes on his plate and Anansi had one.

But Anansi wanted more cakes. He decided to trick Rabbit. He made a scary noise on his big drum.

'Help!' shouted Rabbit *'A monster's coming!'* He ran away and hid under the bed.

Anansi took one more cake and put it on his plate. Now he had two cakes. Rabbit came out from under the bed and looked at his plate. Something was wrong! But before he could say anything, Anansi banged his drum again. Rabbit hid under the bed. Each time, Anansi put another cake on his plate, until all the cakes were on his plate, and none on Rabbit's plate. So Rabbit decided to play a trick on Anansi. He stamped with his strong back legs.

'What's that noise?' said Anansi.

'It's elephant. Watch out Anansi, he might stamp on us.'

'Help!' said Anansi and he hid under the bed. While he was there, Rabbit changed the plates over. Now Rabbit had all the cakes and Anansi had none. Poor Anansi!

Story summary

Rabbit offers Anansi the spider one of his cakes but Anansi wants more.

Anansi frightens Rabbit by making a big noise: while Rabbit hides he moves the cakes, one at a time, on to his own plate.

Rabbit in turn frightens Anansi away and takes his whole plate of cakes back.

back, they can tell him what Anansi has done. At each stage, model the language 'one more', 'one less' or 'one fewer'.

> *One group of children had an interesting response to sharing the cakes.*
>
> *Joshua put two of the five cakes on each place and held the last one up in the air. 'That's the amount they ought to have,' he said. 'Because Anansi has two and rabbit has two.' 'Who has that one?' asked Phoebe, pointing to the extra cake. 'Perhaps rabbit,' says Caitlin. 'Because rabbit is the best.'*

Big questions

- How many cakes on the plate? Why does Anansi want more cakes? Is that fair? Should Rabbit give him more cakes?

- Why is rabbit scared? Are you scared of anything?

- How many cakes on each plate now? Who's got more cakes?

- At the end of the story, what does Rabbit say to Anansi? What does Anansi say to Rabbit? How could we share the cakes fairly?

Example stories from children

Thomas takes the maths of the story in a different direction as he explores the concept of 'just right'.

> ### Thomas' story
>
> *Dough cakes. There is a little cake for bunny. It's perfect for her.*
>
> *"That's perfect" [says Thomas in a bunny voice] She said it's perfect too. It's going to have only one cherry.*
>
> *There's a little pie on her head now! There's one pie on her head and three on the plate. She's in my pocket. She just fits. She loves my lovely pocket.*

Follow-up activities

As extensions to the story, try these variations:

- Anansi asks the children to predict before he moves the cake: *'if I take one more, how many will I have then? Will I have more or will rabbit have more?'*

- Anansi puts the cakes not on a plate but in a bag so they

can't be seen. Can the children work out how many he's got in his bag when they can't count the cakes? What strategies do they use?

- Ask the children to use wooden numbers or number cards to represent how many cakes on each plate. Does this help them spot the pattern that one number goes up as the other goes down?

Make playdough cakes: use buttons or bottle tops as cherries. Rabbit makes a cake each for himself and Anansi and puts the same number of cherries on his cake and on Anansi's. Anansi sneaks an extra cherry so that he has one more. Rabbit has to get another cherry so that it's fair. Model the language 'one more' each time. This was the story two children told in response to the 'cherry' scenario:

> *Anna: Would you like one more cherry, Phoebe? Mine has more cherries on. I know because I looked at it. Look at mine. It's got a tiny shiny cherry in the middle.*
>
> *Phoebe: Mine's got two cherries on. I can put another one on.*
>
> *Anna: It's broken! Mine's broken! One came off! Oh, I'll squeeze it back on.*
>
> *Phoebe: Look. I'll show that to my mum. It's not a cake. It's got smarties on it and chocolate because it's called chocolate cake. It's my birthday next summer. It's birthday cake playdough.*

Circle games

- **Who stole the cookie from the cookie jar?:** give each child a toy animal to hold. Using the the rhyme below, invite the children one at a time to let their toy sneak a 'cookie' out of the jar. Count to see how many have gone and how many are left.

- **Elephant on a spider's web:** using the rhyme below, invite the children to add elephants one by one to a spider's web made of string. Or use real children, and invite them to walk around the spider's web. Each time, one child chooses a new friend to join them on the web, until the last verse – when they all fall down.

Daily routines

- When children are getting ready for something, e.g. putting on their socks and shoes, keep a running total with the children of how many people are ready.

- Buying apples in a role-play shop, adding carriages to a train track – all kinds of games offer an opportunity for using the language 'one more' in a meaningful context.

Outdoor activities

- **Play long jumps:** put out one log and ask the children who can jump over it. Put out 'one more' next to it and ask

who can jump over both logs together. Continue adding 'one more' log and get the children to see how many logs they can jump over. Ask them to make marks to show how many they jumped over.

- **Train game:** the children find a space to be their 'train station'. One child is the train and goes round the outdoor space stopping at each 'station' and picking up a passenger, counting how many on the train each time.

Using ICT

- The iPad app 'Cupcake design' (see Further resources) allows children to play out this story, and offers lots of opportunities to use the language 'one more, one less'.

- Young children love to play with calculators, and often use a great deal of mathematical language if they are able to use them in role play, for instance in a pretend office or shop. But if they press [+1] they can turn the calculator into an adding machine: each time they press = the number changes. They could use the '+1' machine to keep a count of how many cakes are being added on to a plate, but they are more likely just to see how far they can count and how fast they can press the buttons. Try starting at 100 and making a '-1' machine. What happens when they get to zero?

Younger children

- Offer a bag of exciting toys and a box. Invite the child to take the things out of the box one at a time, modelling the phrase 'one more'. When they have finished playing, help them put the toys back in the box one at a time.

- Build a tower of blocks for the child to knock down, saying 'one more' as you add on another.

Footprints in the sand

Mark-making

Set up an obstacle course for bikes. Offer some children clipboards and helmets to dress up in. Every time their friend completes one circuit on the course they can make 'one more' tick on the sheet.

Assessment opportunities

Free play sessions making playdough cakes offer an ideal opportunity for observing children's mathematical language, and the challenges they set themselves. Do the children use the language 'one more?' or 'one less'? Can they work out

how to put a situation 'right' by adding or subtracting?
Do they talk about solutions to problems?

> *Anna spontaneously used counting, subtracting and mathematical language as she played:*
>
> *Anansi's eating. Yum yum yum. 1, 2, 3, 4.*
>
> *He's eaten all the cherries. No cherries left.*
>
> *(Anna makes some more cherries) You can't have these. These are for pudding.*

Links to other parts of the book

This module fits well with:

✓ Number 0: separating groups of numbers different ways

✓ Number 6: adding two groups of numbers

✓ Number 7: mistakes in counting

Songs

'The cookie jar'
Whole group: *Who stole the cookie from the cookie jar?*
(Child X) *stole the cookie from the cookie jar.*
(Child X): *Who, me?*
Group: *Yes, you!*
(Child X): *Not me!*
Group: *Then who?*

Repeat, giving different children a chance to be steal a cookie.

(Source: traditional, adapted from old-fashioned party game)

'One elephant'
One elephant went out to play
Upon a spider's web one day
She thought it was such incredible fun
That she called for another elephant to come.

Two elephants….

and so on until:

5 elephants went out to play
Upon a spider's web one day,
But all at once the web went 'snap'
And the 5 little elephants fell down flat.

(Source: Harrap, B., Sanderson, A. and McKee, D. (1994)
Okki-tokki-unga)

And of course, the perfect counting down song:

5 Currant Buns
5 currant buns in a baker's shop
round and fat with sugar on the top
Along came (Rumi) with a penny one day
Bought a currant bun and put it away.

(Source: traditional, Matteson, E. *This Little Puffin*)

Number Two – Pairs

EYFS Maths Objectives

✓ Begin to organise and categorise objects (Number 16-20 mths).

✓ Compare two groups of objects, saying when they have the same number (Number 16-20 mths).

✓ Solve problems, including doubling, halving and sharing (Number early learning goal).

✓ Recognise, create and describe patterns (Shape, space and measure, early learning goal).

Resources

A playmat or cloth, and a blue cloth for the sea. A boat – which can be just a cardboard box – a collection of animals, four or five pairs, and a single unicorn; or, as it's an imaginary creature, you can ask the children to describe or even draw it.

Once upon a number: 2

For children, two is the number of belonging: two friends, parent and child. It's the number of movement, as the child learns to defy gravity by standing and then walking: the rhythm of up, down, up down, and marching left, right.

The number two is crucial to many areas of mathematics: children building with blocks need two shapes, one on each side, to make a construction balance. Children have two hands, two feet, two ears: looking at the 'two-ness' of their

Into the Ark

A twist on a centuries-old story is ideal for learning about odd and even numbers, pairs, doubling and halving. It is inspired by an inter-faith story, appearing in many cultures around the world. It can also be told without the religious connotations by changing the Mr Noah to a zookeeper rescuing his animals from high water.

Story outline: Into the Ark

'It's going to RAIN,' said Mr Noah. 'We have to build an ark to keep everybody safe.'

'EVERYBODY?' asked Mrs Noah.

'You, and me, and the animals. We'll take two of each kind so that each of them has a friend.'

When the ark was finished, Mr and Mrs Noah started looking for animals to go inside. But Mr Noah could only find one elephant. 'That's odd,' he said, 'There should be two.'

So the elephant trumpeted loudly, and along came another elephant.

'That's better,' said Mr Noah. 'Now there are two.'

Then he spotted a lion: two elephants and one lion – that's three. 'Only one lion? That's odd! There should be a pair.' So the lion roared, and along came the other lion. 'That's better,' said Mr Noah, 'Now there are four.'

He carried on counting the animals, but just when he thought he'd found every one, along came the unicorn. 'Only one unicorn? That's odd,' said Mr Noah.

'Everybody knows,' laughed the unicorn, 'There's only one unicorn. I'm unique.'

'I don't believe it!' said Mr Noah. He went off to look for another unicorn. But while he was gone, the rain started to fall. 'Come along, Mr Noah!' called Mrs Noah, 'It's time to go!'

They forgot the unicorn and sailed off. It came swimming after them, so fast it crashed into the ark and its horn made a hole in the side.

'Dog,' said Mr Noah, 'Go and put your nose in the hole to stop the water getting in.'

So dog put his nose in the hole, but his nose was too small and the hole was too big. The water kept coming in.

Then Mrs Noah went down and put her knees in the hole. But her knees were too small and the hole was too big.

So Mr Noah went and sat in the hole. His bottom was just the right size to stop the water coming in. And ever since then, dogs have had cold noses, girls have had cold knees, and boys like to warm their cold bottoms in front of the fire! But who knows what happened to the unicorn?

Story summary

Noah is looking for two of each kind of animal, but he can only find one – an odd number.

Along comes the second one, and it makes two: an even number.

He can't find a pair for the unicorn, because the unicorn is unique.

own bodies helps them explore the patterns of symmetry. When children organise objects in pairs, they are laying the groundwork for learning about doubling and halving.

Why this story?

Many children love to line things up horizontally: they are often very keen to pair up the animals ready to go in the ark. This is a good story, too, for children who like to explore vertical trajectories as they march up, down. Matching objects in pairs teaches about the patterns of number, the rhythm of counting, as well as about doubling and halving. In this story it's easy to show children how to count in twos, and how to find out how many objects in two pairs, four pairs, six pairs: the beginnings of multiplication. The contrast between the paired-up animals and the unicorn, one of a kind, makes it easy to grasp the concept of odd and even numbers.

The story opens up moral questions about friends, trust, and belonging. It can spark off difficult conversations about whether you prefer to be on your own, or with a friend, what it feels like to be 'the odd one out'. It's an inclusive story to tell when not every child lives in a nuclear family with two parents.

Joining in with the story

Before the story, children can spread out the cloths, deciding which part is water and which is land. They can help 'hide' the animals in the cloth. Involve them in deciding how Mr and Mrs Noah are going to set about building the ark, and mime some of the hard work! You can ask the children to make the sound of the rain, using body percussion or instruments.

Then, one at a time, invite children to help Mr Noah can find them. As the animals come out of their hiding places, there's plenty of scope for making animal noises! Children can take turns lining the animals up ready to go in the ark, counting them at each stage. Ask them to tell Mr Noah whether the animals are all in pairs, or to join in with his puzzled chant 'That's odd! There's one left over.' It becomes easy to see the difference between odd and even numbers.

Big questions

- Do you think the lion likes being on his/her own? How does she feel when she's found a friend?

- Why do you think there's only one unicorn? When do you like to be on your own? When do you like to be with a friend?

- If there are five animals, can they all be in twos, or is there an odd one left over? Two hands: what else have you got two of on your body? What have you only got one of?

- What do you think happened to the unicorn at the end of the story?

Example stories from children

Jasper and Joshua's story

Jasper: I've got two crocodiles. They're biting you. Now they're fixing you. The parrot will fly over the top.

Joshua: I've got the elephants. They're going in. They're all in. Put them in here to carry. Look, they've all gone in now. I can carry many!

Sam's story

I found something. I found water. I'm sinking. The zebras are sinking in the water. The crocodiles are eating the giraffes. Yummy yummy.

Amelia

The animals are going in the ark. Someone's missing! It's unicorn!

Bye unicorn. We're going to put the lid on. Unicorn can go on top.

Unicorn's going to give tiger a ride. Tiger's having a ride he's really lucky. Other tiger comes along. 'I'll give you a ride tiger,' says dog. 'There you go.'

Follow-up activities

Halving and doubling: share a pile of animals between two people: one for me, one for you. Can children guess in advance how many each one will have?

- **Mr Noah can only find one of each animal:** one lion, one alligator, one bear, one elephant. How many does he have? How many will there be when he's found the other animals?

- **Play pairs games:** either commercial board games, or make your own using real objects: toothpaste and toothbrush, bucket and spade.

Odd and even: whisper counting is an easy way of learning to count in twos. Line up the animals from the ark in pairs. Explain that one of each pair is very quiet, and the other is noisy. Count the animals, saying one number quietly and the next one loudly. The children may realise they are saying all the even numbers loudly! Then try missing out the odd numbers entirely.

- **The odd shoes game:** ask the children to take off their shoes and put them in a pile in the middle of the circle. Take out 1 shoe. Ask the children to guess whose shoe it is. 'That's odd! (Child X) would look odd with only one shoe!' Find the pair so that the owner has two shoes. Then do the same thing again with 3 shoes: that's odd: 1 pair of shoes and one left over and so on. Line the shoes up and take turns counting them until all the shoes are accounted for.

Balancing: Mr Noah wants to make the ark balance properly. Help him arrange the animals so that there's one of each on each side of the ark.

- Put the animals on a set of scales, one of each pair in each side of the scales. When there's an odd number of animals, what happens to the scales? Draw a picture of what happens (or what you think might happen) when you put an odd number of animals on the scale.

Patterns: march in a pattern, 1, 2, 1, 2. Make different repeating 1, 2 patterns: a clap and a jump, or a nod and a skip. Extend it to two claps, two jumps. Make patterns with beads or printing shapes.

Symmetry: show the children that they have two hands, feet, ears etc.; one on each side of their body. Ask them to make symmetrical patterns with their body (e.g. by stretching both arms out).

- Put out a piece of string. Put one animal on one side of the string. Ask the children to find the matching animal and put it in exactly the same place on the other side of the string. Continue with more pairs of animals until you have a symmetrical picture. Or do the same activity using pairs of blocks, to build Noah's dream house when the ark comes to land!

Exploring symmetry

Alessandro took two wooden animals and put them together in a symmetrical shape. 'Look!' he said, 'Their legs fit.'

'It looks like a butterfly,' commented his friend Dieneke.

- Take symmetrical photos of objects/animals/children. Cut the pictures in half along the line of symmetry. See if the children can guess what the picture is, and find the matching other half. Or put a mirror down the middle of the picture to find the line of symmetry.

- Fold a piece of paper in half, and cut a pattern down the edge. Open it up, and find a symmetrical pattern. For more able children, fold the paper many times to make a snowflake.

Circle games

Play games where children have to work in pairs:

- **Sing the song** 'Row row row the boat/gently down the stream.' The children sit in pairs facing each other, holding both hands, and rock forward and back in time to the song.

- **Making the bed:** children stand facing each other and hold hands. They chant the rhyme 'Make the bed, make the bed, turn the blanket over.' On 'make the bed', they swing their arms from side to side: on 'turn…' they turn away from each other in a circle without letting go hands – tricky, but it can be done!

- **Dance to country music**, dancing in pairs. Will everyone have a partner, or do you need to have a three? You could give the person left out the privilege of choosing the pair they want to join.

Daily routines

- Ask the children to go into lunch two by two – they could move like animals from the story.

- Ask children to help with jobs like pairing socks and sorting out piles of boots.

Outdoor activities

- Tread in a bowl of mud wearing wellies. Make footprints, walking or jumping, along the ground or a long piece of paper.

- Make a pile of conkers, apples or pine cones, and share it between two people: one for me, one for you…

- Go for a walk along a street and look at the numbers. Do the children notice that they are arranged in twos, all the odd numbers and all the even numbers together? If so, can they count them using the whisper counting they've learnt? (See page 18.)

Using ICT

- Use the symmetry setting on the camera to turn one friend into two, or make funny symmetrical pictures of your friends. Print out some of the pictures and display them: can you work out who is who? Simple matching games on the computer like 'Things that go together' in 'Sherston's Mini-matchers' encourage work on pairs.

Footprints in the sand

Mark-making

- Arrange blocks or toy houses to make a street. Encourage children to make number labels and post them on the houses in the street.

- Ask the children to draw symmetrical pictures on the computer using a drawing programme like 'Revelation Natural Art'.

- Turn a notebook into 'Mr Noah's Counting Book'. Mr Noah has to feed all the animals. Ask the children to make marks in the notebook so he can remember how many animals have already had their dinner. Use buttons or bricks as toy food and match the food to the animal.

Assessment

Let children improvise their own pair stories using the props. Invite them to add wooden numbers to their arrangements of props as they tell you the story. Take photos of the result.

What to look for

Can the children identify even numbers or say when they have a pair of animals? Do they arrange the animals symmetrically?

Younger children

- March to lively music, chanting 1, 2, 1, 2. Count rhythmically, emphasising every other number, as you climb upstairs.

- Young children and babies like to play with mirrors: it's a great moment when they notice that their reflection in a mirror is a copy of themselves.

- The 'copy cat' games that babies and young children like to play – waving goodbye, clapping or babbling

in response to an adult – lay the groundwork for understanding symmetry and pairs.

- Their first shoes, as well, are another powerful experience of 'two-ness'.

Songs

The animals went in two by two

The animals went in two by two, Hurrah, Hurrah,
The animals went in two by two, Hurrah, Hurrah,
The animals went in two by two, Hurrah, Hurrah,
The elephant and the kangaroo,
And they all went into the Ark for to get out of the rain.

The animals went in three by three, Hurrah, Hurrah,
The animals went in three by three, Hurrah, Hurrah,
The animals went in three by three, Hurrah, Hurrah,
The butterfly and the bumble-bee,
And they all went into the Ark for to get out of the rain.

(Source: Traditional Song, see Further resources)

Two little hands

Two little hands go clap, clap, clap
Two little feet go tap, tap, tap;
Two little eyes are open wide,
One little head goes side to side.

(Source: Traditional Song, see Further resources)

Additional stories

- Anno, M. (1999) *Anno's Mysterious Multiplying Jar*

- Cole, B. (2000) *Two of Everything*

- Cousins, L. (2013) *Noah's Ark*

- Pleasant DeSpain (2007) *The Doubling Pot*

- Keen, S. (2012) *Knitted Noah's Ark*

- Lindsay, E. and Sharratt, N. (2013) *Socks*

Links to other parts of the book

This module fits well with:

✓ Number 7: counting

✓ Number 9: pattern

Number Three – Position

EYFS Maths Objectives

✓ Use senses to explore the world around them. (Characteristics of Effective Learning, playing and exploring – see note on shape and space, birth-11 months).

✓ Use positional language (Shape, space and measure 30-50 mths).

✓ Describe their relative position such as 'behind' or 'next to' (Shape, space and measure 40-60 mths).

Resources

An outdoor space with a bridge (which can be a plank or some chalk marks on the ground), a treasure box with three objects in (not necessarily the ones in this version of the story).

Molly Whuppie and the Bridge of One Hair

Outdoors is the best place to tell this traditional Scottish story, which can be used to introduce concepts of position and direction.

Once upon a number: 3

Three is the number of story: three sisters, three treasures, three tasks – beginning, middle and end. In this story there are also three dimensions to explore: forward and back, side-to-side, up and down.

Why this story?

In this story, it is an advantage to be small. Molly Whuppie, the smallest of three, can hide without being seen. She is light enough to run across the bridge of one hair when the giant can't. Children who are the youngest in their family particularly enjoy this story, while those who like transporting

Story outline: Molly Whuppie and the Bridge of One Hair

Three sisters lived in a little house and the youngest was Molly Whuppie. They grew too big for their little house, so they went to seek their fortune. They walked all day and at night they came to a forest. The older two were frightened, but *'I'm not scared,'* said Molly Whuppie.

At last they came to a castle! *'I'm not scared,'* said Molly Whuppie and she knocked on the door.

Inside was a GIANT. *'Fee fi fo fum, a yummy girl for my hungry tum'* he said.

The older two wanted to run away, but:

'Can we come in for tea?' said Molly Whuppie.

The giant was so surprised he let them come in and gave them some tea. After tea he took out his treasure box and counted his treasure: a golden purse, a golden sword, and a golden key.

Then he let them sleep by the fire and he went to bed. Mollie's sisters fell asleep, but Mollie slept with one eye shut and one eye open. In the middle of the night the giant felt hungry. *'Fee fi fo fum, a yummy girl for my hungry tum'* he said, and started to come downstairs.

'Let's get out of here!' said Molly Whuppie. She and her sisters ran away, and the giant ran after them. He ran and they ran, through the forest and over the hill, under the cliff and around the rocks, until they came to the Bridge of One Hair. Mollie and her sisters ran over but the giant was TOO BIG.

He shook his fist at Molly Whuppie: *'You watch out, Molly Whuppie, don't you dare come here again!'*.

'I'm not scared!' said Molly Whuppie. *'I don't like that giant. I'm going to teach him a lesson.'*

So the next day Molly went back across the bridge of One Hair to the giant's house and hid in the cupboard. When the giant went to bed, she crept out and took the golden key from the treasure box. But the lid of the treasure box creaked and woke the giant. He chased Mollie through the forest and over the hill, under the cliff and around the rocks, to the bridge of One Hair but he was TOO BIG to cross.

He shook his fist at Molly Whuppie: *'You watch out, Molly Whuppie, don't you dare come here again!'*.

'I'm not scared!' said Molly Whuppie.

She gave the key to her oldest sister. But the next day she went back to the giant's castle and hid under the table. She stole the golden purse, and the giant chased her through the forest and over the hill, under the cliff and around the rocks, across the bridge of One Hair.

'You watch out, Molly Whuppie, don't you dare come here again!'

'I'm not scared!' said Molly Whuppie.

She gave the purse to her middle sister, and the next day she went back to the giant's house and hid behind the sofa. She stole the golden sword, and the giant was so angry, he forgot that he was TOO BIG. He chased Molly Whuppie right across the bridge of One Hair. The bridge broke, the giant fell in the water and that was the end of him. But Molly Whuppie lived happily ever after with her sisters.

Story summary

Molly Whuppie and her sisters escape from the giant's house across the Bridge of One Hair.

Molly Whuppie goes back three times to steal the giant's treasure, hiding in different places.

The last time, the giant runs after her across the Bridge of One Hair, and falls in the river.

objects from place to place love the game of 'stealing' treasure from the giant.

The story enables children to use all the outdoor space available to them, and climbing areas – in particular bridges – to explore position and direction as they sneak up on the giant and run away. They describe and make journeys, and follow and give directions. They use positional language

when finding hiding places for Molly Whuppie or safe spots to keep their treasure.

Joining in with the story

Joining in with the words is half the pleasure of the story: the giant's *'fee-fi-fo-fum,'* or Molly's cheeky *'I'm not scared,'* as children try out what it feels like to be a huge giant or a small heroine.

They enjoy the rhythm of 'he ran and she ran…', tapping their knees fast for Mollie Whuppie and slow for the giant to make the sound of footsteps.

Make a rhythmic chant of 'through the forest and over the hill, under the cliff and around the rocks' to encourage children to use positional language.

Big questions

● Why do you think Molly Whuppie and her sisters grew so big? Are you growing?

● Where do you think Molly Whuppie's house/ the castle/ the bridge is? Who might live in the castle? What could be inside the treasure box?

● How does Molly/the giant move? Fast or slow? Which way should Molly go to get to the bridge? Why can't the giant get across the bridge of One Hair?

● Where should Mollie hide in the castle? What do you think they will do with the treasure?

Example stories from children

Some children retold the story with puppets in the doll's house. But George and Keir replayed their version of the adventure outside. It fed into their enthusiasm for chase games and their dialogue about 'baddies'.

George and Keir's story

'They heard a noise. It was King Mouse. They ran away through the tunnel and over the rock and round the grass and the trees and over the tall mountain.

I am going to get that King Mouse's sword off him. I'll pull it off him so hard. We're going to get King Mouse. We're trying to throw him in the toilet. "We'll throw you in the toilet now, you wicked King Mouse."

We're going to get some sand and throw it in King Mouse's eyes to be mean to him. He's a baddie. He likes bad things.

It was hard to get King Mouse. I had to go around the rock and then over the grass and then I got to King Mouse's house and I throwed the water and the bucket full of sand. He ran away into his castle. It's got bumpety bits all the way up to the sky.

A story from Rose and friends

Rose: There's Molly Whuppie. She finds her mummy. She says 'There's a monster in our house.' She's going to hide in the cupboard. She's sleeping.

Rohan: She can't get out. I've put her in prison.

Dieneke: What about a blanket in the cupboard. Because she's sleeping.

Sam: Someone's walking about looking for her. It's a mummy. It's not her mummy. It's a mummy wrapped up in bandages.

She's run away. She's got to the bridge. She doesn't fit under the bridge. She'll have to go on top.

Follow-up activities

This story makes a good basis for an interactive adventure outside, including one or more of the following elements, and leaving yourself free to follow the children's story ideas rather than sticking closely to the script. Before you start, ask the children to find three treasures to put in the box. For example, instead of a purse, a key and a sword, a group of children found a stick, a stone, and a small rake from the sandpit and told me about their magical properties:

'That stick's a wand! It can turn you into a frog or a lion.'

'It's a magic stone. It can turn into a star. It can do anything.'

And as for the rake: *'It can hurt you. It can rake you. It can make you dead. The other end can make you better.'*

Setting off: let the children choose a place to be Mollie's house, and a place, not too close, to be the giant's castle. See how many people you can fit inside Mollie's house – you can have many more brothers and sisters than in the original story! Explain that Molly Whuppie is growing. For example: 'I'm growing,' said one child. 'I've got big legs. They're growing so long.' 'I'm getting big,' said another. 'Because I'm eating so much. I'm going to be a grown-up.' They agreed the house was now too small. 'We're off to look for a big high up tall house.'

Ask one child to be Molly Whuppie and lead the way as you set out to seek your fortune. Everybody else lines up behind them, following the leader. Molly Whuppie has to walk in a straight line until s/he comes to an obstacle. The group tell her which way to go: 'This way/left/backwards/over/under'. Keep going until you get to the 'giant's castle'.

In the giant's castle: take turns being Molly Whuppie knocking on the door and the giant answering. Ask the

children to help count the treasure (giants are notoriously bad at counting). See if the children can remember what treasures are in the giant's box.

Running away: model the directions from the giant's castle to the bridge, based on the children's earlier ideas: 'over the log', 'around the sandpit'. If the children enjoy 'giant' games, the adult can act out being the giant shaking his fist as the children run over the bridge. Find a safe place to sit down and get your breath back. Then invite individual children to have a go at retracing their steps to the giant's castle, stealing the treasure and running back, guided by the group who give them directions: *'I'm climbing down the bridge, I'm going through the tunnel and that's where you get to the giant's house.'*

Ending the story: leave it to the children to decide what Mollie and her sisters will do next. Suggested endings have included Molly Whuppie making friends with the giant or Mollie's brothers turning into superheroes who go looking for treasure of their own.

Other scenarios also offer dramatic play and also encourage children to use positional language:

- The giant is trying to think of different places to hide his treasure chest. Working in pairs, the children can take turns hiding the treasure and then giving their friends instructions to find it.

- Hide the 'Molly Whuppie' doll in the doll's house. Give the children instructions about where to look: 'under the bed' 'in the bath'. Then let them give the instructions.

Rose hid the doll for her friend: 'Is she on top of the light? Is she in the bathroom? Is she under the toilet lid? Open the lid, Alessandro. Look inside. Is she behind the chair? Is she under the blanket? It's mummy and daddy's blanket. I've put it on their bed.

- Put a 100 square that is printed on clear acetate, over a picture of Molly's forest. Work out which numbers Mollie has to travel along to get home.

Circle games

- **The 'creep-up' game:** one child is the giant. S/he spreads out several musical instruments as 'treasures' in front and then pretends to go to sleep. The other children take turns to creep up, steal one of the treasures and hide it. The giant has to guess which treasure has gone and describe, from the sounds they heard, where they think it is hidden.

- **Position 'Simon says':** ask each child to stand on a mat. Ask them to jump behind the mat, in front, to one side, to the other, to walk all around it, and so on.

- **Robot walk:** ask children to walk like a robot, at first forward and back, then introduce turning left and right. Use arrows signs to prompt them. Invite them to give directions to their friends.

- **Dance the 'Macarena':** to practice jumping a quarter turn to face in a different directions. Apart from anything else, it gives young children (and adults) a chance to make mistakes joyfully! (There are several versions on YouTube but check them out properly first.)

Daily routines

- Send children on errands, for instance, to fetch something or put it away in a particular place. Give directions using mathematical language: 'Can you put the teddy next to my chair?'. Try using two prepositions: 'Can you find the pot of chalks on top of the table behind the sellotape?'.

Outdoor activities

Many of the previous activities are best done outside. As in George and Keir's case (page 23), the story can help to make repetitive chase games more complex and mathematically interesting.

- The same positional language can also be used in **obstacle courses**. Provide a selection of 'obstacles' – balancing beams, logs, or just mats and blankets. Allow children to help set up the course, deciding which obstacle to put where. Use chalk arrows to give directions.

- **The wellie direction**. Position wellies around the outdoor space. The children have to walk in the direction the wellies are pointing to reach the next pair of wellies. Can they follow the wellies and get safely back to the beginning of the course?

Using ICT

- Use a programmable toy such as Beebot™ to navigate a path through a floormat 'forest'. You could hide 'treasures' in the forest for Beebot™ to collect.

- Find Internet pictures of familiar objects taken from an unusual angle. Ask children to say if you are looking from 'above' or 'below'. Invite children to take their own peculiar photos – underneath the water tray, perhaps, or behind the sofa, saying which angle they took them from.

Younger children

- Give children opportunities to go over, under and round obstacles. Turn a walk into town into an obstacle course: go round the post box, under the underpass etc. On the way home, ask children which way to go.

- Notice children's awareness of where things are. Can they unerringly find the biscuit tin, and do they know where to look for a favourite toy?

- Use an instrument to make noises in different places and see whether the baby or child will turn their head to look for it.

Footprints in the sand

Mark-making

Make maps of the outside area: either use photos to make a simple map for the children to follow or allow them to make their own. Ask them to colour in all the places they think are 'dangerous' and 'safe' in different colours. Get children to take you on a tour of dangerous places, drawing a line to show your route.

Assessment opportunities

- **'Talking Box' games:** use two bags of identical props. Sit opposite a child with a screen in between. Ask the child to copy what your verbal instructions, without seeing what you are doing on the other side of the screen: 'put the doll on the chair' 'put the red block next to the blue block'. Take the screen away and see if the two layouts are the same.

- **Opposites game:** use a commercial game, picking out

cards that use positional concepts: in and out, or up and down – or make your own.

What to look for

What positional language does the child use when following and giving instructions? Do they also use this language in free play?

Songs

A Mouse Lived...
A mouse lived IN a little hole
Lived softly in a little hole
When all was quiet as quiet can be
OUT popped he!

A mouse lived UNDER a little house...
A mouse lived BEHIND a little tree...

(Source: adapted by the author from traditional rhyme)

Little Peter Rabbit
Little Peter Rabbit had a fly upon his nose,
Little Peter Rabbit had a fly upon his nose,
Little Peter Rabbit had a fly upon his nose,
So he flipped it and he flapped it and the fly flew away.

Try these additional verses: 'a fly behind his ear'/'a fly under his chin'/'a fly inside his shoe'.

(Source: traditional, Matteson, E. *This Little Puffin*)

Additional stories

- Berenstain, S. and J. (1981) *Bears in the Night*

- Brown, R. (2010) *Snail Trail*

- Fanelli, S. (1995) *My Map Book*

- Goodhart, P. and Sharratt, N. (2004) *You Choose!*

- Mizielinska, A. and Mizielinski, D. (2013) *Maps*

Links to other parts of the book

This module fits well with:

✓ Number 10: 100 square

✓ Number 13: size

Number Four – Shapes

EYFS Maths Objectives

✓ Notice simple shapes in pictures (Shape, space and measure, 22-36 months).

✓ Show an interest in shapes in the environment (Shape, space and measure, 30-50 months).

✓ Talk about the shapes of everyday objects (Shape, space and measure, 30-50 months).

✓ Select a particular named shape (Shape, space and measure, 40-60 months).

✓ Explore characteristics of everyday objects and shapes and use mathematical language to describe them (Shape, space and measure, early learning goal).

Little Piece

This is a story about 2D shape recognition, tessellation, and fitting in with a group.

Resources

A collection of shapes – circles, triangles, squares and rectangles – and boxes or trays to sort them into. A bag with one of each shape plus a hexagon and one piece from a simple jigsaw. Turn shapes into instant puppets by drawing a face on each one.

Once upon a number: 4

Four beats in a bar, four directions of the compass, four sides and four corners to a square: four is a strong and important number in the mathematics of shape and space. A 'square' number, 22, 4 is the smallest number of objects that can be arranged to make a square. This story introduces four common shapes in early years maths – circle, triangle, rectangle and square – and uses numbers to describe them: counting edges, circles, the number of shapes you need to put together to make a bigger shape.

Story outline: Little Piece

Little Piece was all on her own. She went walking around the world looking for a friend. She met Circle. *'Can I play with you?'* she asked.

'Yes!' Come and play! We're playing rolling around,' said Circle.

Little Piece had a go at rolling around, but it wasn't easy.

She met Triangle. *'Can I play with you?'* she asked.

'Yes!' Come and play! We're playing holding hands and pretending to be a square,' said Triangle.

Little Piece liked holding hands, but she didn't look much like a square.

She met Square. *'Can I play with you?'* she asked.

'Yes!' Come and play! We're playing at building roads,' said Square.

Little Piece joined in, but her bit of road was lumpy.

She met Rectangle. *'Can I play with you?'* she asked.

'Yes!' Come and play! We're playing stretching up tall,' said Rectangle.

But Little Piece didn't have long sides like the rectangles.

She started to cry. *'I can't play any of those games!'* she said.

Along came wise old Hexagon. *'Let's play making pictures'* he said.

All the shapes made pictures together and Little Piece was in every picture.

They made pictures until it was bedtime. The circles rolled away. The triangles, the squares, the rectangles and the hexagons all fitted together, with no gaps.

'I wish I fitted in like that,' said Little Piece.

'Somewhere,' said the wise old Hexagon, *'There's a family waiting for you, too, Little Piece.'*

Just then she heard some voices shouting. *'Little Piece! Little Piece! There you are! We've been looking for you everywhere! We can't finish the jigsaw without you.'*

And Little Piece went to join her jigsaw friends, all different shapes and sizes, just like her.

Story summary

Little Piece can't join in the other shapes' games because she isn't the same as them.

Old Hexagon suggests they play at making pictures, all different shapes together.

Finally Little Piece finds a jigsaw that needs her to complete it.

Why this story?

This story encourages children to look closely at 2D shapes, not just to learn their names, but the mathematical language needed to describe their properties: corner, edge, straight, curved. It also explores the things that each shape can do, both on their own and in combination with different shapes. Sorting the shapes will appeal to children who like to arrange objects in grids; other children will enjoy exploring circles and rolling.

Children in an educational setting begin to learn useful lessons about how to be part of a group. They watch what their peers are doing, and work out how to behave like them. They look at their friends' body shapes and features, clothes and toys. They find out about when they need to fit in, and when it's ok to be different.

Joining in with the story

Before the story, if necessary, introduce all the shapes, asking the children about their properties. Look at the number of corners. Look at the different kinds of edges: straight, curved, long, short. Use the word 'edge' rather than 'side' to avoid confusion when you move on to 3D shapes, which have both sides and edges.

The children can guess the shapes in the story as each one is introduced (see the 'Shapes in a Bag' game, on page 28). They can play the 'shape games' in the story: rolling circles, arranging triangles to make a square shape, and so on, as well as helping to make pictures.

When the shapes all go to bed, the children can sort them back into the right places. Finally they can decide where Little Piece fits in with the rest of the jigsaw.

Big questions

- Why can't Little Piece roll? What other shapes can roll? Can circles fit together with no gaps? Why not?

- Can you make two triangles look like a square?

- What shape can two squares make together? Why can't Little Piece make part of a road?

- Which are the long sides of this rectangle? Who do you think Little Piece should play with?

- What games do you like to play with your friend? Is your friend like you? Is he/she different? How are they different? What can your friend do that you can't? What can you do that your friend can't?

Example stories from children

Boris

Boris, worked out that diamonds tessellate. He added several to his picture and said: 'Look what I did. It all fits together. It looks like an arrow.'

Maja

Maja, who has only just begun to speak English, collected a lot of circles and showed them to me.

'I made a story: look! This is my picture. Where they go? This way or this or this? (she arranged the collection of shapes in a circle)

They go this and this and this and this. It's going in… a circle.

Now they going away to their sleeping place. I need more circles.

Adam and Han Chong

Adam carried on adding squares to the road in the story. 'Look, I made a road. It goes all the way down there and then it goes back.'

Han Chong said, 'A road needs a car!' He picked up a diamond shape and 'drove' it along the road.

Martha

Martha acted out her story energetically.

'There's the sun. Two suns! I'm making the grass. Little Piece is jumping. That's a trampoline.'

Follow-up activities

These activities can also happen before or during the story.

Unfolding the cloth: use a square or circular cloth to put the story props on. Begin with the cloth folded up, and ask the children about the shape as you unfold it.

As an example, children gave these descriptions of the circular cloth as it unfolded from a thin segment to a whole circle: *"It's a bit of an icecream/ It's a tree. It's a tent/ It's a triangle. It's a pushchair [cover]. It's a moon/It's a semi-circle/It's a circle!/It's the moon too"*. They enjoyed predicting what would happen as we unfolded the square: *'it's going to be another square' 'it's going to be a rectangle.'* Adam noticed the repeating pattern – rectangle, square, rectangle, square.

'Shapes in a Bag' game: put 5 or 6 flat shapes in a bag. If necessary, put matching shapes visible near the bag. Bring one of the shapes very slowly out of the bag, so that you can only see a tiny part of the shape. Ask the children to guess which one is coming out. Can they say how they knew? This is quite hard for young children: Adam said *'It's a circle! Because it's got this!'* and drew a curved edge in the air. As more of the shape emerges from the bag, they may change their minds. Lorelei guessed: *'It's a square! Because it's got four sides'* (even though she couldn't see all four sides) and then as more of the rectangle emerged, she guessed the rectangle correctly: *'Because it goes like this!'* and she stretched her hands high in the air to show that the rectangle was tall.

Use an enticing selection of shapes to encourage free play and picture-making. Include shapes in different colours and textures: see-through glittery gel shapes for the light box: flat regular shaped objects – a coaster, a paperweight, a set square: or laminated pictures of shapes in the environment: a manhole cover, a window, a triangular roof.

Tessellation games: put tessellating shapes in a mirror box and encourage children to start their tessellating patterns in the corner, so that they can see their pattern reflected in three dimensions. See if they can use just one shape: triangles, or squares, for instance, and then offer more than one shape – for instance triangles and rectangles.

Spot the missing shape: press small 2D shapes into flat tiles of dough. Take one away without the children seeing. Can they guess which one has gone?

Make patterns with circles using natural objects: orange slices, slices of tree branch, round seed heads.

Make angular patterns with shiny metal parts from a hardware store: round washers, triangular brackets, hexagonal nuts and so on. Or square patterns using mosaics as an inspiration: Roman mosaics, or a Gaudí mosaic dragon.

Circle games

- **Touch something round:** this game is great for getting people moving, even in a crowded space. Ask children to go and touch something round, square, rectangular,

something with curvy sides, the corner of something. Some children may have trouble finding shapes: pair them up with a friend to begin with, or suggest places to look.

- **Body shapes:** hold up a shape. Ask children to make the shape with their bodies: legs astride to make a triangle, or thumbs and fingers put together to make a square. Encourage them to extend their bodies and make big shapes. As an extension, ask them to work in pairs: can they work together without words?

Daily routines

- This shape-inspired rhyme is good for loosening up, shaking out the fidgets and getting focused:

  *'Wide as a gate: tall as a house
  Thin as a pin, small as a house.'*

  Do the rhyme all the way through, then call out the actions in a random order. Or make your own version with the children.

Outdoor activities

- **Go on a shape hunt:** give each child a different shape and ask them to see where they can see them in the garden, or on a walk in the street. Some are easier to find than others! Take pictures of some of the shapes they find and make your own shape book.

- **Shark attack:** put out large shapes as stepping stones. Can the children jump from one to another? Can they jump only on the triangles? Only on the squares? Invite some children to be 'sharks' swimming around in the sea. Tell the other children they can only escape the sharks by standing on circles/rectangles etc.

Using ICT

- Cut a square or circular piece of paper into several pieces. Put it back together again and take a picture. Bit by bit move the shapes outward away from each other, taking a picture each time. Put all the pictures together and you have a movie of your shape exploding! On a tablet, use a time-lapse photography app like 'IMotion' from Fingerlab.

Younger children

- Give babies pictures and mobiles to look at with sharply defined black and white images. This helps them to focus on shapes and the lines enclosing them.

Footprints in the sand

Mark-making

Drawing shapes is a lot harder than recognising shapes. Encourage mark-making with fingers in different multi-sensory textures: a sand tray, a tray of glitter, in cornflour and water slime, or a patch of mud. Copy the marks children make, then invite them to copy your shape. Talk through how you make the shape 'down, along, up and back across the top' to help them focus more consciously on what they are drawing.

Assessment opportunities

Encourage children to make their own 'Little Piece' pictures with 2D shapes. Take photos of their pictures and record their stories.

What to look for

Are the children interested in playing with shapes? Do they name simple regular shapes? Do they talk about their properties, using words like 'corner' 'edge' 'straight' 'curved'? Do they talk about what a shape looks like – an ice cream cone or the the sun, for example? Do they use shapes in their pictures based on what their properties are?

Songs

Little Piece has her own theme tune, from Robert Schumann's 'Album for the Young': www.youtube.com/watch?v=y-vrkhZwwqM

My hat it has three corners: a song about a triangular hat! (from *Okki Tokki Unga*, by Harrap, Sanderson and McKee)

Shape song
(to the tune of 'Do you know the muffin man')

Do you know what shape this is,
I'm holding in my hand?

I have got a triangle, a triangle a triangle
I have got a triangle
I'm holding in my hand.

(Source: adapted by the author from the traditional rhyme)

Sing the 'shape version' of The wheels on the bus

The wheels on the bus go round and round...
The windows on the bus are square square square...
The door on the bus is a rectangle...
The wipers on the bus make a triangle...

(Source: adapted by the author from traditional rhyme: original version in Harrap, B., Sanderson, A. and McKee, D. (1994))

Additional stories

The story in this chapter is inspired by Leo Lionni's classic book:

- Lionni, L. (2012) *Pezzettino*

Links to other parts of the book

This module fits well with:

✓ Number 8: 3D shape

✓ Number 9: pattern

Number Five – Counting

EYFS Maths Objectives

✓ Count an irregular arrangement of up to ten objects (Number 40-60 mths).

✓ Count objects or actions that cannot be moved (Number 40-60 mths).

✓ Know that numbers identify how many objects are in a set (Number 30-50 mths).

✓ Recite some number names in sequence (Number 22-36 mths).

Resources

Natural materials – wood, stones, leaves etc. – that can be used to make features of a landscape, a set of five dinosaurs plus a little green frog.

where to stop when counting – and it has a lot of scope for getting things wrong.

Once upon a number: 5

Five is a powerful number for children to use when exploring calculation and counting, because it lends itself to the best mathematical apparatus in the world – fingers. They have been exploring this maths resource since they were a few weeks old, and they don't get lost! They understand that however you arrange them, there will still be five. And because it's an odd number, however you partition them, there will be different

The Five Foolish Dinosaurs

The many different versions of this old folktale involve camels, donkeys or fishermen; but a set of knitted dinosaurs inspired this variation. Despite the slightly complex joke at its heart, it's a simple story which helps children understand the concept of the last number in the set. It gives them practice in learning

Story outline: The Five Foolish Dinosaurs

One day five little dinosaurs went off to play in the swamp. *'Be careful,'* they said to each other, *'make sure nobody gets lost.'*

They played all day, and at the end of the day, Pterodactyl said *'Let me count and see if all our friends are still here!'* So she flew to the top of the tree and began to count.

'Big Plesiosaur beside the rocks, that's one.

Little Plesiosaur behind the log, that's two.

Green Stegosaurus between the grasses, that's three.

Brown Tyrannosaurus in the mudpatch, that's four.

Four! That's only four! We've lost one of our friends!'

But big Plesiosaur said: *'Perhaps you've counted wrong. Let me try!'*

So big Plesiosaur counted.

'Purple Pterodactyl up the tree, that's one.

Little Plesiosaur behind the log, that's two.

Green Stegosaurus between the grasses, that's three.

Brown Tyrannosaurus in the mudpatch, that's four.

Four! That's only four! We've lost one of our friends!'

Each of the dinosaurs tried to count, and each could only count four friends. They started to cry. *'We've lost one of our friends!'*

'What's the matter?' asked a voice from the swamp. It was Little Green Frog. *'Let me count for you'* she said.

'Big Plesiosaur beside the pond, that's one.

Little Plesiosaur under the log, that's two.

Green Stegosaurus between the grasses, that's three.

Brown Tyrannosaurus in the mudpatch, that's four.

Purple Pterodactyl up the tree, that's five! Five dinosaurs. You're all here.'

The dinosaurs thanked the Little Green Frog for finding their lost friend. They never got lost in the swamp again.

Story summary

Five dinosaurs go to play in a swamp.	Each dinosaur counts to see if all their friends are there, but thinks one is missing because they forget to count themselves.	Little Green Frog counts all the dinosaurs. They realise there were five of them all along.

numbers in each set – 3 and 2, or 4 and 1. Many number rhymes use 5 objects, for example. '5 little ducks', '5 speckled frogs'. In the UK, for children in the first year of school, reaching the age of 5 is a milestone.

Why this story?

Counting and re-counting scattered children is a familiar scenario for any adult who has ever taken a group out on a trip. The story shows children how counting can help them stay safe, and make sure that they are with their whole group. It gives children experience in counting random arrangements of objects, and emphasises the 'cardinal principle': the idea that the last number counted is the number of the whole set.

As the children count the dinosaurs they use mathematical and descriptive language to describe position (in the mud, behind the rocks).

It's a good story for children who like to make collections of things or hide things in holes, as well as for those who love dinosaurs.

Joining in with the story

Before the story starts, arrange the resources with the children and let them decide what the features of the swamp will be:

'That could be the dirty ground'

'It's rocks... those are stepping stones.'

'There's a fish and whale and snake in the sea.'

'There's a wriggly worm.'

Invite them to choose a dinosaur and give it a name or a description: the Purple Pterodactyl, the Green Tyrannosaurus. Count the dinosaurs, inviting the children to join in, at the beginning of the story, to establish that there are five. Model counting strategies that the children will find useful, such as pointing to the dinosaurs while counting: marking the starting place so that nothing gets counted twice: or keeping a tally on your fingers.

Help children understand the importance of the last number in the set by repeating it emphatically *'1, 2, 3, 4, 5 – five, That's five dinosaurs.'*

When the dinosaurs take turns to count, the children enjoy joining in with the rhythmical words: 'one on the log, that's one….' Ask the children what the dinosaur has done wrong. Once the children have spotted that the dinosaur is forgetting to count itself, do it again, once or twice, so that all the children have a chance to spot the mistake and enjoy the joke.

Ask them to join in the correct counting at the end of the story.

Big questions

- What's different about each of these dinosaurs? Where would the dinosaurs like to play? What might they do there?

- What different ways can you think of to count the dinosaurs? What's gone wrong? How could they put it right?

- How many dinosaurs are there really? Are they all there? How did you work that out?

- Why should they make sure everyone is there? How do they feel when they think one of their friends has gone?

Example stories from children

Joshua brought a fire engine along to listen to the story. He made the fire engine ladder into a bridge and put a dinosaur on one end.

Joshua's story

'Him falling down a bridge. He's the same. He's blue.

Him friends falling down to the bridge. Him didn't fall down him helped the people.'

Jasper and Atlas' story

Atlas chose three dinosaurs. 'They're the same. They're all green' He hid them in the water. 'They're hiding. You can't see them.'

Jasper: 'This is the baby dinosaur. There's no sister. This is the big brother and the mother. These are stepping stones: spread it out a bit [the cloth representing the river.]'

Atlas: 'It's a Diplodocus. It's the same as Jasper's Two Diplodocus. He's in the sea. He goes in the mud. He's stuck. This one can eat all the mud and get him out. It's eaten all the mud. It's yummy.'

He piled them up. 'They're in a tower. The big brother's at the bottom, because he's strong.'

Amelia was keen to tell a story using the 'swamp'. She enjoyed behaving like a 'teacher' as she told her story.

Amelia's story

'I'm going to get my story giraffe and tell a giraffe story.

'Here they are. Which one of them is the biggest? Yes. And which one is the smallest?

'Is this a cool giraffe? It's really soft. Now feel this he's even softer.

'There's a little giraffe and a big giraffe helping her and they both played in the mud together (she talked in role) "I'll help you, little one."

Thomas' story

Thomas, an able mathematician, loved the 'silly counting.' He counted 5 dinosaurs accurately, then started to play about with numbers. He made his dinosaur count '1, 2, 3, 4:100!' and then '100, 400, ten hundred.'

Follow-up activities

The mother dinosaur has laid some eggs. The little dinosaurs hide the eggs to keep them safe. Then Mother dinosaur asks the little ones to bring the eggs home.

Can the children remember where they all are? Is there one egg for each dinosaur?

Sam loved this story. He looked for the eggs and matched one egg to each dinosaur.

Circle games

- Using the song 'The Pigeon House' (see opposite), ask the children to stand in a circle and link hands. Choose four or five children to be 'pigeons'. The children in a circle raise their hands and the 'pigeons' run out between them and find a place to perch. Ask the remaining children to check: can you see all the pigeons? Do we have the right number?

  At the end of the song, the pigeons come back and pretend to sleep. Check that we have them all again. Swap over so that everyone has a turn being a pigeon, or give the children toy birds to use as props during the song, and count them all in and out.

Daily routines

- Many settings incorporate counting into their daily routine. How many children are here today? How many cups do we need to get out? Are all the bikes back in the shed? But what happens if you sometimes vary the way you count: Is it the same number wherever you start? Is it easier to count children in a circle or a straight line?

Outdoor activities

- **Take the children out:** to a forest, park, outdoor space where they can run freely. Allow children to share the responsibility of making sure everyone is there and nobody is missing.

- **Play hide and seek:** count how many children you've found and how many you still have to find.

- **Hide dinosaurs in the sand pit:** tell the children how many dinosaurs are hidden and ask if they can find them all. Let the children take turns in hiding the dinosaurs for each other, and make marks to record how many dinosaurs are found.

Using ICT

- Try the counting app, 'Jelly Bean Count', which encourages using fingers to count (see Further resources).

Younger children

- Offer babies different sets of objects to explore: sometimes use all the same object, like a sorting set of dinosaurs, sometimes a collection of different objects.

- Hide a collection of objects around the room. Can the children find them? Can they hide them for you to find?

'I've got four eggs. There's one more. I'm checking in the mud. One more egg is missing. The dinosaurs are checking everywhere they can't find them.

One of the dinosaurs is missing. I can't find them. There's one under there. There's one more. No, there's two. That one hasn't got an egg and that one has, so one egg is missing. We need one more for that one. And two more are missing because that one hasn't got one. Yeah, two is missing. One more egg! Now we have one more egg for her. We made it! We can eat them.'

Dinosaur families: the dinosaurs are going home to bed, each with their own family. Ask the children to sort them into sets and count how many in each family. But in the middle of the night they all sneak out to play. Muddle them up together (perhaps sneakily hide a few). Wise old Diplodocus calls them home. Can the children sort them out again and check whether there are still the right number?

Wrapping paper counting: give each child a square of wrapping paper with pictures of lots of different kinds of dinosaurs (or any other objects) on them. Who's got the most pterodactyls? The fewest tyrannosaurus? Encourage them to set their own counting challenges.

(Age 3+ only) Put a see-through tray on a light box. Arrange coloured sand and shiny glass beads for 'jewels'. Provide small baskets so that children can find and collect treasure. They can draw in the sand to make marks to record their treasure.

- Play finger rhymes, counting fingers and toes, such as 'This Little Piggy went to Market' or 'Round and Round the Garden'. The sense of suspense as you walk your fingers up the baby's tummy – 'one step, two step' – lays the groundwork for future counting games.

Footprints in the sand

Mark-making

- To make sure that none of the dinosaurs are missing, invite children to make a map of the swamp and mark where the dinosaurs are.

- Make a box of 'treasures'. Take some photos of the treasures altogether for the children to use as a 'checklist'. Hide the treasures around an outdoor space. Can the children find them all and check that they are all there? Can they use a blank piece of paper and find their own way of recording the treasures they have found?

- Hide dinosaurs in a sand tray. Ask the children to draw dinosaur tracks or footprints to show where each dinosaur has gone.

Assessment opportunities

Take pictures of the children's own arrangements of the dinosaurs from their stories/small world play. Invite them to talk about the pictures, describe where the dinosaurs are, and count how many are there.

What to look for

Can children count a collection of objects without moving them? What strategies do they use? Can they talk about what they did?

Songs

The Pigeon House
My pigeon house, I open wide,
And set all my pigeons free.
They fly all around
And up, and down
And light in the tallest tree.
And when they return from their merry, merry flight,
They close their eyes and say "Good night"
Coo-coo-coo-coo, Coo-ooh-coo-ooh-ooh-ohh
Good night!

(Source: traditional http://guidingjewels.ca/resources/songs/620-song-my-pigeon-house)

Ten big dinosaurs (Sung to: '10 Little Indians')
1 big, 2 big, 3 big dinosaurs,
4 big, 5 big, 6 big dinosaurs,
7 big, 8 big, 9 big dinosaurs,
Ten big dinosaurs!
They all lived a long, long time ago.
They all lived a long, long time ago.
They all lived a long, long time ago.
Now there are no more.

(Source: www.bry-backmanor.org/dinosaurs/dinosongs.html)

All around the swamp
(Sung to: 'The Wheels on the Bus')
The Pteranodon's wings went FLAP, FLAP, FLAP,
FLAP, FLAP, FLAP, FLAP, FLAP, FLAP
The Pteranodon's wings went FLAP, FLAP, FLAP
All around the swamp.

The Tyrannosaurus Rex went GRRR, GRRR, GRRR,
GRRR, GRRR, GRRR, GRRR, GRRR, GRRR,
The Tyrannosaurus Rex went GRR, GRR, GRR,
All around the swamp.

The Triceratops horns went POKE, POKE, POKE
POKE, POKE, POKE, POKE, POKE, POKE,
The Triceratops horns went POKE, POKE ,POKE,
All around the swamp.

The Brontosaurus went MUNCH, MUNCH, MUNCH,
MUNCH, MUNCH, MUNCH, MUNCH, MUNCH, MUNCH
The Brontosaurus went MUNCH, MUNCH, MUNCH,
All around the swamp.

(Source: www.bry-backmanor.org/dinosaurs/dinosongs.html)

Additional stories

- San Souci, R. and Kennedy, D. (2011) *Six Foolish Fishermen*

Links to other parts of the book

This module fits well with:

✓ Number 0: arranging objects in different ways

✓ Number 3: position and direction

✓ Number 7: mistakes in counting

Number Six – Comparison

EYFS Maths Objectives

✓ Categorise objects according to properties such as shape or size (Shape, space and measure, 22-36 months).

✓ Make comparisons between quantities (Number 22-36 mths).

✓ Use vocabulary involved in adding and subtracting. (Number 40-60 mths).

✓ Find the total number of items in two groups by counting all of them (Number 40-60 mths).

✓ Using quantities and objects, add and subtract two single-digit numbers (Number early learning goal).

Lucky Bird Huma

This story about collecting eggs explores different ways of making six, adding, comparing and subtracting different quantities.

Resources

A collection of patterned eggs, egg boxes, and baskets for sorting the eggs. My sorting set of eggs includes six each of stone, wooden, and papier mâché eggs. But dyed hardboiled eggs or painted stones work just as well, or tissue paper eggs made with the children. Improvise a colourful bird puppet with a handful of feathers, or a feather duster.

Once upon a number: 6

Six divides neatly into different sets – two sets of three, three sets of two.

It is also the number of holes in an egg box. The simple egg box makes mathematical operations easy for children to visualise: adding, partitioning and all the mathematics involved in comparing two sets of objects.

Story outline: Lucky Bird Huma

Once there was a poor woodcutter and his wife. They were so poor they had holes in their clothes, holes in their shoes, and no food in the house.

One day, the woodcutter was asleep in the forest. Lucky Bird Huma flew by, looking for someone to help. She landed beside the poor woodcutter and laid a beautiful egg as a present. The woodcutter took the egg home to his wife. He asked her what they should do with this precious egg.

His wife said: *'If only Lucky Bird Huma would live with us, she would lay us lots of eggs, not just one.'*

The next day, when Lucky Bird Huma flew by, the woodcutter called out to her *'Please, Lucky Bird Huma, won't you come to our house?'*

To begin with, the woodcutter and his wife treated Lucky Bird Huma well. But every day they wanted more and more eggs. Lucky Bird Huma laid jewelled eggs patterned with bright colours. She laid shiny stone eggs. She laid smooth wooden eggs. Every day the woodcutter and his wife collected the eggs in baskets and boxes and counted how many eggs they had to take to market to sell.

One day, Lucky Bird Huma stopped laying eggs. Her feathers grew dull, and lost their colours.

'What's wrong, Lucky Bird Huma?' asked the woodcutter.

'I am ill,' said Lucky Bird Huma. *'I need to go outside in the fresh air.'*

So the woodcutter took Lucky Bird Huma outside. At once she spread her wings and flew away. And the woodcutter and his wife never saw her or her eggs again.

Story summary

Lucky Bird Huma lays an egg as a gift for a poor woodcutter.	The woodcutter catches Lucky Bird Huma and forces her to lay him lots of eggs.	Lucky Bird Huma escapes and the woodcutter gets no more eggs.

Why this story?

Children love to collect treasure and fill containers, and especially with eggs, which are little treasure boxes on their own. This is a story about the delight of collecting, sorting, and arranging treasure. It's also about the danger of hoarding precious objects instead of treating them with respect.

Joining in with the story

The children can take turns choosing which egg Huma 'lays', sorting them into different baskets and boxes. They often use rich and varied language as they talk about the eggs:

'This one's a shiny one.'/'This one's a star one.'/'That one's the beautifullest one. I chose this because it's got pink flowers on it.'

Offer them challenges as they compare the eggs in the baskets, using some of the questions opposite.

Keep the numbers small, so that the children can concentrate on the mathematical problems rather than counting.

Finally, sort all the eggs into three egg boxes to make sure you still have three sets of six.

Dieneke and Joshua struggled with questions of size, as well as how to sort the eggs. 'This one is no good and we have to change it. This one is too big and we have to throw it back,' said Dieneke.

'This is where the big one goes,' suggested Joshua, 'And that is where the patterny one goes and that's where the heavy one goes. That one is quite stony. That one is quite patterny. Let's put it with the patterny ones.'

Big questions

- What did the precious egg look like? Which of these eggs do you think looks precious?

- What could the woodcutter do with the egg? Is it right to make Lucky Bird Huma lay so many eggs? Lucky Bird Huma feels ill: what will make her better?

- Which eggs go together? Why? How many eggs in this box? How many in that one? Which has more?

Fewer? Which eggs are there most of? How many eggs altogether?

Example stories from children

Phoebe and Joshua's story

Phoebe and Joshua set their own challenges as they played with the eggs.

Joshua They're eggs. They're for her. [the bird]

Phoebe: They've been laid by my bird. She's called Daisy. Can you hear that sound? She's singing. I'm putting some in the egg box. There are 4. There are 2 holes. Now there's only one hole. Now I've got so many!

This one's almost the same but it's brown. Look, there's five. We need 1 more. These two are littles. These are big. One and two. We need to take these two out [because the lid won't shut].

Joshua: You can have this one!

Phoebe. This one won't fit. There's two holes now. Two. Now it's all full. It's shut. We're all done.

Rosie's story

This is Lucky Bird Huma and these are all her eggs. Lucky Bird Huma can fly 'flutter flutter'. So Lucky Bird Huma took all the eggs and tried to carry them all around the world. Oh no she's lost three.

Joshua: Lucky Bird Huma these are your eggs.

Rosie You've ruined it, Joshua, I'll have to find them again. (She hid the eggs and found them again.)

Then she dropped them, crash, and they cracked. Then the eggs breaked and it was her lucky day they werefull of chocolate.

The eggs are: blackish greyish smooth brownish pinkish peach brown plastic – no it's wood.

Follow-up activities

Adding two groups: the children can roll a die (start with one marked with only numbers 1, 2, 3) and collect the right number of eggs. Then roll again and collect some more eggs from a different basket. How many of each type? How many altogether?

Adding by counting on: repeat the game above, but this time put the eggs in an egg box and close the lid. Remember how many eggs are in the box: the children could make marks on sticky notes to help them. Then when they get the second lot of eggs, see if they can work out how many they have altogether without opening the box. This step into thinking about number in a more abstract way can be quite hard. To make it easier, for instance: if there are three eggs, tap the box three times, counting 1,2,3, and then carry on counting the second lot of eggs.

Saying how many more to reach a given number: Lucky Bird Huma has hidden the eggs all around the house. The woodcutter has to find enough eggs to fill his box. Ask the children to count how many holes in the box. They can go and find eggs, one at a time, to put in the box. At each point ask how many are in the box and how many they still have to find. This is easy, as they can just count the holes in the egg box.

Sam worked out how many eggs in his box with help from a friend.

Sam: 'Can I count? 1, 2, 3

Amelia: 'No, it's 4'

Sam: I'll count again.' He counted 4 correctly. I added in two more eggs and asked: are there still 4?'

Sam: 'No! I'll count! I'll count again! – it's 6!'

Partitioning groups: it's easier for children to understand the relationship between adding and subtracting if they do the two activities together, so try some 'giving away' games.

Lucky Bird Huma has a basket of 6 eggs. She gives some away to her friends. The children can ask for which eggs they want, e.g. '2 patterny and 1 wooden one.' Count how many she gives away and how many she has left. As in the game above, count the eggs, but then sometimes cover up the basket so the children have to guess how many eggs are left. Many experiences of this kind will teach the children that taking away 2 eggs from 4 is a similar kind of problem to adding 2 eggs to 2 more.

Dieneke and Joshua made their own version of this game, with a naughty crocodile stealing eggs.

Dieneke and James' story

The birdie's going to fall down. She hurt herself. She's left her eggs.

James: He [The crocodile] wanted to get the eggs. He took 3 eggs.

Dieneke: My birdie wanted a stone egg. She's going to eat it. She ate it all.

James: (looks at the eggs in a bowl) She's got too many eggs. 6 eggs. There's no room. We need something else.

(He gets an egg box and shares the eggs.) Now there's eggs for the birdie and the crocodile.

Circle games

- **'Stand up if you…':** this is a game about comparing sets. Call out: 'Stand up if you like bananas/if you have black hair/Velcro shoes'.

  Each time, count how many children are standing up and how many sitting down. Then count how many children all together. Use some visible categories (clothes, physical features) and some invisible (likes, ways to travel to school, etc.) The game helps children think about the ways they are the same and different from their friends, and helps them feel accepted in a group.

Daily routines

- **Sharing fruit** is a great opportunity for adding and subtracting. Two apples and 3 oranges, how many is that? 4 pieces of banana, how many more for everyone to have one? If Elly and Rasik each have one of the strawberries, how many are left?

- **Tidying activities:** ask the children to put the red and yellow beanbags in separate containers, and the big and small books on different shelves. Tidying up activities: ask how many they have altogether. Put labels with numbers on storage units, for example: '3 big balls and 2 little balls', '4 pots of crayons and 1 pot of chalks.' Or ask the children to make their own labels.

Outdoor activities

Offer children egg boxes to collect treasures in outdoors. Provide natural objects for them to hide and collect: pinecones or large beach pebbles from a garden centre (suitable for 3 yrs +).

- Provide small bowls/twists of hay or grass to make nests. Fill them with eggs rolled out of clay, or use pinecones.

- Invite children to hide their nests of pinecones round the outdoor space for their friends to find. Challenge them to see how many pinecones they can pick up against the clock.

- Add egg boxes to a mud kitchen, with natural objects to make pretend eggs.

- Write mud kitchen recipes for children to follow, using small quantities of different objects: 3 twigs and 4 conkers. 2 pine cones and 5 leaves.

- Encourage them to 'write' recipes of their own, to add to a 'mud kitchen cookery book'.

Using ICT

- Use a computer game which allows the child to position objects in a landscape – like Sheppard Software's preschool 'Animal Jungle' – to compare quantities of objects: 'Do you have more birds or monkeys?'. 'How about if you took two of the monkeys away?'

Younger children

- For many toddlers, 'more' is a first word! Young children have a good sense of 'less' and 'more': which plate has the most food on, whether their friend has more toys than them. All kinds of experiences, from choosing a plate of fruit, to putting toys in a box and emptying them out again, will help them develop an awareness of sorting and comparing groups of objects.

Footprints in the sand

Mark-making

Offer sticky notes when the children are playing with collections of eggs so that they can annotate how many eggs they have.

Set up a table-top farm shop and ask children to keep track of how many eggs of each different kind they have sold. Offer them price tags, till rolls, order forms to record the information on.

Some settings have the opportunity to show the children eggs hatching in an incubator. Children look really closely at the eggs and the new chicks, and are usually motivated to draw what they see. Their drawings are often quite mathematical, as they try to represent how many eggs they have and how many chicks have hatched.

Assessment opportunities

Have an Easter egg hunt outside. Give each child an egg box to fill. Check with them to find out how many eggs they have and how many they still need to get.

What to look for

Can children compare and count numbers of eggs? Do they do it spontaneously, or only when asked? Do they set their own problems, and reason about numbers? – e.g. 'There's two empty spaces, so I need two more.'

Songs

Here are two rhymes for practising combining groups of objects:

5 Little Soldiers
5 little soldiers standing in a row
(hold up 5 fingers)

2 stood straight and 3 stood so.
(hold 2 fingers straight and 3 crooked)

Along came the sergeant, and what do you think?

They all straightened up as quick as a wink.

Repeat with different combinations of number bonds, or use 10 fingers instead of 5.

(Source: www.rhymestore.com)

Here comes the bus
Here comes the bus, it's going to stop
4 go below, and 2 on top
How many waiting at the stop?

(Source: Brian Hunt, *Count Me In*)

Additional stories

- The original text of the story: http://www.pitt.edu/goldenfowl

- Biro, V. (2013) *The Goose that Laid a Golden Egg*

- Gravett, E. (2011) *The Odd Egg*

- Nicoll, H. and Pienkowski, J. (2011) *Meg's Eggs*

> ## Links to other parts of the book
>
> This module fits well with:
>
> ✓ Number 1: adding on 1
>
> ✓ Number 2: counting in 2s

Number Seven – Counting

EYFS Maths Objectives

✓ Recite some number names in sequence (Number 22-36 mths).

✓ Develop an awareness of number names (16-20 mths) (and recognise the rhythm of counting through songs and repetitive language).

✓ Count objects to 10, and beginning to count beyond 10 (Number 30-50 mths).

✓ Count on or back to find the answer to a problem. (Number early learning goal).

Monkey and the Stepping Stones

This is not just another story about counting. It's about making mistakes in counting, which is mathematically much more interesting, and also guaranteed to make children laugh.

Resources

The story needs pebbles for stepping stones, sticks for crocodiles and a collection of toy monkeys.

Once upon a number: 7

Seven is a number used often in folktales: the hero is often the youngest of seven sons or seven daughters. A distant journey goes over 7 seas or 7 mountains.

There are many groups of seven objects that children are asked to count: seven colours in the rainbow, seven days in the week.

It's a useful number for this story, since most under-5s can't recognise a group of seven objects at a glance, but will have to count them.

Story outline: Monkey and the Stepping Stones

A family of monkeys once lived on an island in the middle of the river, and the youngest was Tumbili. All summer long they jumped across the seven stepping stones, counting as they went – 1, 2, 3, 4, 5, 6, 7 – to reach the fruit trees on the shore and eat the ripe mangoes.

But Tumbili found it hard to count. When he made a mistake, he fell into the water with a splash.

Sometimes he counted like this: 1, 2, 3, jumping up and down on the same stone.

Sometimes he counted like this: 1, 2, 3, missing out lots of stones.

Sometimes he counted like this: 1, 3, 7, 10, missing out numbers.

And sometimes the numbers got jumbled up completely: 8, 2, 5, 7, 9, 4.

Every day Tumbili practised counting. He was sure he would get it right one day.

But one day the water rose and covered the stepping stones. Seven crocodiles came swimming down the river. Tumbili didn't know how to get across. He didn't want to get eaten by the crocodiles.

But Tumbili called out to the crocodiles. *'Oh crocodiles, I have a message for you from the king of the crocodiles. He wants to know how many crocodiles swim in his river.'*

The crocodiles didn't know how many of them were swimming about.

'Don't worry,' said Tumbili. *'I am the king's crocodile counter. Line up in a row and I will count you.'*

So the crocodiles made a line from the island to the bank. Tumbili jumped from one crocodile head to the next, calling out 1, 2, 3, 4, 5, 6, 7 in the right order and he got safely to the other bank.

Story summary

Tumbili the monkey makes mistakes counting the stepping stones across the river.

The floods wash the stepping stones away and bring the crocodiles down the river.

Tumbili makes the crocodiles line up to be counted. He gets across by jumping on the crocodiles as he counts them.

Why this story?

Looking at the mistakes in counting is a powerful way of exploring the many different aspects of counting and the complex skills involved. What's more, it encourages children to use their mistakes as valuable tools for learning. In this story, counting is used for different purposes: not just to find out how many objects there are (the cardinal aspect of counting); but also (in an ordinal way) to measure and label objects, and to mark where the monkey is on his journey.

To count, children have to combine many skills – physical coordination and memory as well as mathematical understanding: and asking them to explain some of the many possible mistakes they can make in this complex process helps them unpick the skills involved.

This story can be used to introduce children to many things that number lines can do: counting forwards and backwards,

beyond tens or twenty, starting and stopping in different places, counting in twos or tens. It's a great story for children who like to connect objects together, and order them in lines and rows.

It also allows children to think about the different kinds of cleverness: the monkey may have trouble learning to count, yet he is cleverest of all because he manages to outwit the crocodiles!

Joining in with the story

The children can help place the seven stepping stones across the river. Count the stones with them to establish firmly that there are seven. When Tumbili's counting goes wrong, the children will correct him gleefully. Some of them may be able to explain what the mistake is.

The story demonstrates the most common mistakes in counting: counting the same object twice, missing out an object, missing out numbers, and saying number names in the wrong order.

If the children choose twigs or knobbly sticks to represent crocodiles, they will have control over the scary part of the story, making it less alarming. Alternatively, substitute hippos for crocodiles.

At the end of the story, when Tumbili has jumped successfully across the stepping stones: children can make the other monkeys jump across, if necessary asking the whole group to help them count.

Big questions

- **Ask questions that encourage counting for a reason:** Amy said 8 stones: was she right? Are there enough sticks for everyone to have one? Are there more crocodiles or more monkeys? Which number do you think Tumbili will get to before he falls in?

- **Questions about counting mistakes:** Did Tumbili count that right? What went wrong? How should he have counted? How do you feel if you make a mistake?

- **'Feelings' questions:** What did Tumbili do that was clever? Was he clever because he counted, or because he tricked the crocodiles? What things do you like to count? What's the biggest number you can count to?

Example stories from children

Isabella

I'm going to tell a story about a crocodile who eats the monkey all up. Over the hills lives a little crocodile called Bing and he wants to eat the monkey. Over the hill he goes and then he goes over the bridge and over the other bridge and over the other bridge... He goes over all those bridges: it's 5!

'He's too quick' says the monkey.

'I'm going to eat the monkey!' says the crocodile.

(Isabella takes the 'bridges' away one by one, counting each time to see how many are left).

Erik

Erik gets out a box of small rubber animals. 'It's the zoo.' He arranges them painstakingly along the edge of a bench. 'They're all there now. They're all in the zoo.' He starts counting them. '12, 13: I got it wrong! I have to start again.'

Another child comes past and knocks some of the animals over. 'Oh no! they've fallen over! You've got to help me stand them up. It's got to be a line.' He carries on counting repeatedly, with his friend helping him.

Follow-up activities

Pebbles are a good way of introducing the idea of a number line. Paint numbers on the stones, or get the children to write numbers on for you, and arrange them in the right order. **Safety:** make sure the pebbles are large enough not to be a choking hazard for the children you work with.

Number lines don't always start from one. Can the children still count along them if they start from 2? From 23? Can they start at number 5 and go on to number 12?

How do the monkeys get home again? Can the children count backwards? If they count backwards from 3, what happens when they get to 0? Negative numbers are supposed to be a difficult concept for children to grasp, but in this context they can be surprisingly straightforward.

Board games are an excellent way to get children counting. Look for simple ones, using coloured spinners instead of dice, or use your own. Dice games are more complicated because they require children to count twice: first the dots on the dice, and then steps along the board. They can be made easier by using dice numbered 1-3, or magic beans (see page 44).

Magic beans: paint 6 butter beans on one side with red nail polish. Put them in a pot. The children shake them out of the pot, and count how many land red side up.

Make a counting book based on a favourite rhyme: for example, a group of children acted out the rhyme '5 little monkeys jumping on the bed' (see page 45), using a sofa instead of a bed. We took a photo each time another child jumped off, and printed out the pictures to make a book. The children enjoyed re-reading it, singing the song as they turned the pages.

The 7 challenge: ask children to roll two dice and count how many dots they get each time. How many times do they get the number 7?

Circle games

- **'Please Mr Crocodile':** mark out two lines for 'banks' of a river. One child stands in the middle as Mr Crocodile. The others line up on the bank and chant:

  Please Mr Crocodile,
  May we cross the water,
  To see our lovely daughter?

  The crocodile chooses a category: 'Yes, if you're wearing blue/have curly hair/like pizza'. The children in that category run across and the crocodile tries to catch one to be the new crocodile. When they reach the other bank,

they count to see how many have crossed over safely and how many are left on the far bank.

Daily routines

- Counting is excellent for moments when children need to wriggle and move their bodies: ask children to join in a rocket launch count down, before jumping in the air. Or count drum beats: then ask them to jump, hop, or stretch in time to the drum beat. This gives valuable practice in physical and mental coordination, as they learn to stop counting and to stop jumping at the same time.

Outdoor activities

- **Role play:** you may have a real puddle that the children can cross on real stepping stones – logs, paving stones, or props suggested by them. How many will they need to cross safely? Will their paving stone be strong and stable enough? How can they help their friends get across?

- Even on a dry day, **a small-world puddle** can be decorated with pebbles and greenery: sticks wound with green wool can make crocodiles.

- **Draw a chalk track** on the ground and model how to write numbers on it – children love long tracks with big numbers. Some children may want to experiment with simple games of hopscotch.

- When moving along a number track, children often mistakenly count the number they are standing on as the first number in the count. They count the squares, rather than the movements. If the numbers are spaced out, so that they have to jump to reach the next one, this will help them focus on counting the jumps, rather than the squares.

Using ICT

- **Counting for a purpose:** encourage children to take part in the UK's Big Butterfly Count (www.bigbutterfly count.org/about) and practise counting moving objects with Inclusive Technology's Touch Balloon programme (www.inclusive.co.uk).

Younger children

When we count steps, jumps and hops, we are linking the rhythms of language and counting to the rhythm of movement. Clapping along to number rhymes, chanting 'one, two, three, go' are all important ways of helping children prepare to learn counting skills. Examples:

- Heather as a toddler loved to count. She counted random numbers as she walked up a flight of steps: 'one, two, eight, seventeen, three...'. Her mother joined in joyfully with the wrong numbers.

- Baby Evie wanted to use a mobile phone like her mother. So her mother loaded an app that makes a sound every time Evie swipes the phone (Fisher Price baby: www.fisher-price.com/en_gb/GamesAndActivities/AppsPage/index.html# but there are many others too). It may only be a small step on the road to counting, but it stops her putting the phone in her mouth!

- Beginning to crawl, Evie follows a trail of toys, pushing each one out of her way, until she finds the toy she wants at the far end.

Footprints in the sand

Mark-making

Often just pen and paper, or chalk on the ground, in the right context, will encourage children to make mathematical marks. For example, James said: *'Let's have a competition to see who's the best at counting stones,'* and started to write the numbers down. *'I've written all the numbers all the way to ten. How do you do eleven? Is it 1,1? How do you do twelve?... Is the next one 1 and 3? Is that thirteen?'* Gripped by the excitement of writing numbers, he carried on to 27.

Assessment opportunities

Make your own board game, drawing a track with as many numbers as you would like the children to explore, and encourage the children to illustrate it with scenery – trees, flowers, buildings – or obstacles and dangers – crocodiles, rivers, or aliens. Some of them may want to make their own board games, writing their own invented marks and numbers.

What to look for

Can children recite numbers in order? Can they count with one-to-one correspondence? Can they recognise when they've made a mistake and work out what went wrong? Can they order or write numbers?

Songs

There's a wealth of traditional counting rhymes, for instance: '1, 2, 3, 4, 5, Once I caught a fish alive', or '1, 2, buckle my shoe'; or for a rhyme related to the story, try:

5 little Monkeys
5 little monkeys jumping on the bed
One fell down and bumped his head
Mummy phoned the doctor and the doctor said
'No more monkeys jumping on the bed.'

(Source: traditional)

Additional stories

- Fusek-Peters, A. and Montgomery-Higham, A. (2003) *Monkey's Clever Tale*

Or try these counting stories:

- Browne, E. (2003) *Handa's Hen*

- Jay, A. (2008) *Counting*

Links to other parts of the book

This module fits well with:

✓ Number 2: counting in 2s

✓ Number 5: counting arrangements of objects

✓ Number 10: counting higher numbers

✓ Number 11: counting out

Number Eight – Shapes

EYFS Maths Objectives

✓ Use blocks to create their own simple structures and arrangements (Shape, space and measure, 16-26 months).

✓ Categorise objects according to properties such as shape or size (Shape, space and measure, 22-36 months).

✓ Show interest in shape by sustained construction activity or by talking about shapes or arrangements (Shape, space and measure, 30-50 months).

✓ Explore characteristics of everyday objects and shapes and use mathematical language to describe them (Shape, space and measure, early learning goal).

✓ Order two items by weight or capacity (Shape, space and measure, 40-60 mths).

✓ Use mathematical names for 'solid' 3D shapes (Shape, space and measure, 40-60 mths).

Resources

A collection of different shaped packets, tins and boxes, wrapped up in colourful paper – different size cubes, cuboids, triangular prisms, and cylinders. It's an even more useful resource if the boxes are filled with different amounts of materials such as sand, cotton wool, beans and rice, old keys. Children are really surprised to find a small shape that is heavier than a large one: and they all make interesting sounds, too, when shaken. This story also needs a sack and a slope for rolling (made out of a board and some blocks).

The Lost Parcel

Christmas and birthdays, and any other festivals or celebrations involving parties and presents, offer a good opportunity for exploring 3D shapes and their properties.

Story outline: The Lost Parcel

Father Christmas was tired. He stopped for tea at his friend the Tooth Fairy's house. He left his last sackful of presents in the sleigh.

But while he was inside, the Tooth Fairy's pet mice came out and nibbled a hole in the sack with their sharp white teeth. When Father Christmas picked up his sack, the presents dropped out. Some of them fell on the ground, but some of them rolled to the bottom of the hill.

'Oh no!' said Father Christmas. He picked up some presents and put them back in his sack. He didn't noticed that some of them had rolled to the bottom of the hill. He got back in his sleigh and drove off, leaving some of the presents behind!

But the Tooth Fairy's mice, with their sharp little eyes, saw the presents rolling past. They ran to the bottom of the hill and picked them up.

'I think this one's got dancing shoes in it. It must be for Cinderella.'

'And this one could have a frog-sized crown in it. Perhaps it's for the Frog Prince.'

The mice delivered all the presents to the right people. The last present was a big round cheese. I wonder who that was for?

Story summary

Father Christmas has a hole in his sack and the presents fall out.

Father Christmas picks them up, but doesn't notice that some of them have rolled down the hill.

The mice find the missing presents. They guess what's inside and deliver them to the right people.

Once upon a number: 8

Just as four was a useful number for talking about 2D shape: eight is important for 3D solid shapes. It is the number of edges and corners on a cube, cuboid or box shape.

It's a significant number for mathematicians, as it can be divided again and again: 2 x 2 x 2, or 2 cubed.

Why this story?

Christmas is a perfect time to explore 3D shapes, when children are interested in parcels and presents. But the story setting can easily be changed to a birthday or other festival, with an over-worked postman instead of Father Christmas.

A wrapped-up present is an invitation to think about shape: if you look at a wrapped up ball, you think about it being a sphere, instead of something to play football with. It's the perfect story for children who like enveloping and wrapping things up!

Joining in with the story

Children love to play with the presents in this story. Spend a good while 'packing' Santa's sack before the story starts, allowing the children to pick up and handle the presents,

compare them, talk freely about them and suggest what might be inside them. If they do not have very much experience of opening presents, you might want to model opening a present, talking about the shape and size, wondering what might be in the parcel and who it might be for.

Let them take the 'dropped' presents out of the sack, one at a time. First ask them to predict whether or not the present will roll, and then they can try it out for real on the ramp. (If your hill is too steep, some of the flat-sided presents will slide!)

Then, like the mice, they can guess what's inside a present, and who it might be for. At the end of the story, get them to put the presents away (see the 'back in the sack' game).

Note: The children need to know that these are only 'pretend' presents, or they won't stay wrapped up for long.

Big questions

- What shape have you got? Is it big or small? Heavy or light? How many corners does it have? Does it have straight or curved edges? How many edges?

- Is your present like any of the others? What's the same about them?

- What sound does it make? What do you think is inside it?

- Why was Father Christmas tired? How did the mice feel when they saw the presents rolling down the hill? Why did they deliver the presents?

- How did Cinderella feel when she got her present?

Example stories from children

Liam's story

Liam took the smallest present from the sack. He played at hiding it and then finding it in different corners of the role-play area. Then he came to show an adult: 'Look at this!'. He'd discovered that his present just fitted inside a little round pot. Florence commented: 'It's because the present's so little. Because the pot's round and the present's square.'

Andrew's story

Andrew piled all the presents into the sack. When one of the children complained, he said, 'I want to be father Christmas. I need all the presents in the sack.' His friend saw the logic in this and helped him collect all the presents.

'I'm going to give all the presents to the people,' he said. 'You have to be asleep to get presents.'

The other children curled up in corners in the role-play area and pretended to be asleep. Andrew and his friend tiptoed round, telling everyone sternly to keep their eyes shut, and delivered the presents, discussing who would get which present.

Follow-up activities

Talking about shapes: invite children to take a present out of the sack, to handle it, turn it over, feel the edges and corners, shake it to see what sound it makes. Encourage them to say what they notice about its shape, size and properties, modelling mathematical vocabulary. Allow them to play freely with the shapes: their talk will often be more productive than if they are asked to comment individually in a formal way. Finally, put the presents down all together. While the children shut their eyes, take one away. Can they describe the one that is missing?

Florence chose one shape: 'because it's the shiniest.' She shook it: 'It makes a noise! I think there's stones inside all of them'.

Anya looked at the wrapping paper: 'It's got squares on it. Just squares. Squares all over'.

So did Timothy: 'It's got circles on. It's for mummy. I'm giving mummy a treat'.

Mathematical vocabulary: introduce words to describe the properties of the shapes: big and small, curved and flat, corner, edge, and face, ('side' can be misleading because it can refer to the edge or to the flat face). Use the conventional names for solid shapes: cube, cuboid (or box), cylinder, triangular prism: but also accept the names that children to come up with themselves. Their language is often rich and wide-ranging, not restricted to mathematical terms.

Han Chong wasn't confident at speaking out in a group, but he showed by pointing that he recognized mathematical language e.g. squares, circles, longer, taller.

In contrast, Caleb was keen to show off his knowledge. 'It's got two circles, one at each end. This bit is curved like the earth. Because the whole earth does go round, did you know that?'

Both children were showing their interest and engagement in different ways.

Back in the sack: each child takes a present out of a hole in the sack. Santa comes looking for the lost presents. He describes each present, (e.g. 'it's tall, it's got a circle at each end and a curved surface, it's big and covered in spotty paper) and the child holding that present puts it back in the sack.

Making sets: Jack writes to Santa. 'I only like presents that have square faces.' Can you help Santa sort the presents into shapes that Jack wants, and shapes that Jack doesn't want? Count the two sets at intervals to see which set has more. Repeat for other types of shape – the children can choose the category.

The 'next to' game: each child takes it in turn to take a present out of the sack and arrange it in a circle. They have to say something that is the same about their present and the present next to it, e.g. 'they're both tall'/'they both have curved edges'/'they're both wrapped in spotty paper.' End up with a circle where each present has one thing in common with the present next to it.

'Next to' people: take the game further by extending it to people. Can the children think of a way they are a little bit like the person next to them? Size, hair colour, clothes? And what ways they are different?

Weighing presents: 'My sack is too heavy!' says Father Christmas. 'I'm going to leave all the heavy presents behind.' Children take it in turns to pick two presents, guess which is heavier and which is lighter, then use the scales to check.

Wrapping up presents: get a variety of boxes and packets and lots of cheap wrapping paper. Children can make and wrap pretend presents. Encourage them to talk about what shape and size of paper they need, as well as what they will pretend is inside their parcel and who they will give it to.

Circle games

- **The feelie bag game:** put some objects that are regular 3D shapes – a ball, a building block, a rolling pin, etc. in a bag. Pass it round a circle, singing the song 'Here's a bag to feel inside' (see page 50). At the end of the song, the child holding the bag puts their hand in the bag and finds a shape. Can they describe it without taking it out of the bag?

Daily routines

- Putting away blocks is a great activity to get children talking about shapes, especially if they have to match the blocks to a 2D outline on a shelf.

Outdoor activities

- Take the present wrapping activity outside. Provide brown paper, tape and string for children to wrap parcels. They can make marks on the parcels and use trolleys and trucks to 'deliver' them. Use bigger boxes and make towers and stacks of them.

Using ICT

- Take photos of children building a construction from blocks – or encourage them to take the pictures. Help them to put the pictures together in a slide show, so they can see a fast-forward version of their building activity. Encourage them to talk about what they were doing, which blocks they used, and why.

Younger children

- Before children can name shapes confidently and talk about their properties, they need lots of experiences with different shapes of objects, regular and irregular, shapes with corners and shapes that roll, and chances to stack, build and balance. Involve them in 'tidying' the kitchen cupboard and playing with pots and pans. Let them climb into boxes, bowls and tunnels to explore 3D shapes from the inside!

Footprints in the sand

Mark-making and recording

- Children's block play creations are the best evidence of their experience of 3D shapes, especially if you can record what they say as they work. Try giving them clipboards and pens so they can record their creations by drawing them.

- Look at the unusual 3D creations of the Dutch artist, Escher, and use them to inspire the children's drawings of their own creations. His pictures are often drawn from an odd perspective, from down below, or a bird's eye view from above. Or use pictures of castles or unusually shaped buildings as an inspiration.

Assessment opportunities

- The best time for talking about shapes is when children get into trouble with their model-making: when yoghurt pots won't stick, or the sellotape gets tangled. Recycled materials often present problems which children can't solve on their own, giving adults a chance for a conversation about shapes and their properties that's meaningful to both partners.

What to assess

What language do children spontaneously use when they talk about shape? Can they predict how solid shapes will behave – for instance which shapes will roll, and which will make a firm base for a tower? Can they say what properties shapes have in common? Do they choose shapes carefully when they are building with them?

Songs

Feelie bag
Here's a bag to feel inside,
Something here that likes to hide
Wide or narrow, short or tall,
Can you guess its name at all?

(Source: Nicolls, S, (1992) *Bobby Shaftoe clap your hands*)

Come to the party
Come to the party, Come to the party
Come to the party, Come right now

Think of something you want to do
And you can do it right now.

You can wrap presents on your own,
You can wrap presents with a friend
You can wrap presents with everybody
And you can do it right now

(Source: Powell, H. (2013) *Game Songs with Professor Dogg's Troupe*)

Additional stories

More ideas of maths activities with presents are available from:

- http://nrich.maths.org/content/id/9720/Presents.pdf

- Baal-Teshuva, J. (2002) *Christo and Jeanne-Claude on unusual things to wrap up*

- Escher, M.C. (2008) *Graphic Work mind-games with 3-D shapes*

Classic storybooks featuring presents:

- Ahlberg, A. and J. (2013) *The Jolly Christmas Postman*

- Burningham, J. (2004) *Harvey Slumfenburger's Christmas Present*

- Briggs, R. (2013) *Father Christmas*

- Campbell, R. (2013) *Dear Santa*

- Dr. Seuss (2003) *How the Grinch Stole Christmas*

- Ray, J. (2012) *The Twelve Days of Christmas*

Acknowledgment: the story and related activities in this chapter have been influenced by the work of Zoe Rhydderch Evans on soft play maths.

Links to other parts of the book

This module fits well with:

✓ Number 3: position

✓ Number 4: 2D Shape

Number Nine – Pattern

EYFS Maths Objectives

✓ Notice simple shapes and patterns (Shape, space and measure, 22-36 months).

✓ Recognise, create and describe patterns (Shape, space and measure, early learning goal).

✓ Use familiar objects and common shapes to create and recreate patterns (Shape, space and measure, 40-60 mths).

Resources

A set of different colour scarves tied together to make the snake, a collection of soft toy birds, including a black and white loon, a strip of white cloth and a set of lolly sticks to make the pattern on the snake.

Once upon a number: 9

The Rainbow Snake

This colourful story introduces different aspects of pattern: not just colour, but patterns of sound and movement.

The rainbow snake story encourages children to look at colours in the world about them and also to arrange colours in patterns on the snake's long twisting body.

Seeing patterns in number is at the core of learning mathematics. From arranging colours and shapes in repeating patterns, children move on to thinking about patterns in number. Nine is a number that lends itself exceptionally well to patterns. A square number, it can be arranged in three rows of three.

It is also three times through a sequence of traffic lights, red, yellow, green: or three repetitions of a clapping pattern: clap, tap tap, or jump, clap clap.

Story outline: The Rainbow Snake

Long ago in the Amazon rainforest, they say, the birds spent their days flying around, high up, low down, this way and that. In the evening they came home and talked about all the colourful things in the world that they'd seen.

But way down at the bottom of the Amazon river, the rainbow snake loved the colours too. He took some colours, bit by bit, to decorate his white snakeskin.

One day the birds saw that all the colours had disappeared and the whole world was grey: grey trees, grey flowers, even grey birds. They decided to go and look for the lost colours.

The birds looked high up, low down, this way and that: but they couldn't find any colours. One by one they came back. Only the loon, the bird with the crazy voice, wasn't there. The birds called her but she didn't answer. She just kept on looking for the colours.

At last she came to a deep river. She plunged down, down, to the bottom. There she saw the rainbow snake. He had all the colours of the world wrapped around him in wonderful patterns.

She came back and called her friends with her crazy screeching voice, and they all answered. *'Help me get the rainbow snake up from the bottom of the river!'* she said. *'We'll come!'* they said.

So all the birds followed the loon to the Amazon river and dived in.

Each of the birds picked up a part of the snake in its beak. The brave loon took the snake's black head. Together they lifted the snake out of the river and up into the sky. But as they rose above the water, they began to pull in different directions. The snake curved right across the sky, stretching thinner and thinner. The colours fell from his snake skin and rained down on the earth in every direction. The birds were each left holding a scrap of a different colour in their beaks. And those are the colours the birds wear to this day: the blue jay, the yellow-hammer, the red kite.

The loon was plain black, because she had been holding the black head. But the birds gave her a present: a beautiful silver necklace. To this day she wears the necklace and she still dives to the bottom of the river. And to this day you can sometimes see the rainbow snake in the sky.

Story summary

The rainbow snake steals all the colours from the world.	The loon is the only bird who finds out where the colours have gone.	The other birds help her lift the snake into the sky and get back the colours.

Why this story?

There are many types of pattern in the story. There are line patterns – curvy, zig-zag, straight – on the snake's back; patterns of movement, as the birds fly up and down, this way and that; and patterns of sound – the songbird's call answered by the loon's crazy screech.

Like many popular folktales, the story has a moral about working together and sharing. It's also about different ways of enjoying colour, whether in a wild profusion in the environment, or organised into regular patterns and shapes.

Children with grid schemas will be keen to arrange the colours in regular patterns on the snake's patterned back: children with trajectory schemas will enjoy flinging the colours back into the sky.

Joining in with the story

At the beginning of the story, the children each choose a bird toy. They 'fly' them around, copying the pattern: up, down, up down, or forwards, back, forwards, back. They can talk about the colours they can see around them, for example: *'I see red, orange, purple, blue.'/'I love blue. I love green and blue.'*

The children can arrange coloured lolly sticks on the white cloth to represent the patterns on the snake's back. For example, one group explored the shapes they could make with lolly sticks as well as colours: *'I made a door!'/ 'I made a fence.'*

Finally, the scarves are tied together loosely to make a multicoloured snake, and passed around the circle, so that each child is holding a piece. They lift the snake together in the air and, as they stretch, the scarves burst apart and fall on the ground. The children look at the colours on the ground and say what colour their bird matches.

Big questions

- If you were a bird, flying around outside, what colours do you think you might see?

- Why does the snake want the colours? How do you think he arranged the colours on his coat?

- Why has the world gone grey? Can you always see bright colours, or do things ever look just grey?

- Is it fair that the snake has all the colours? How could the birds get the colours back? Is it fair to take all the colours away?

- What colour is your bird? Which bit of the snake do you think it was holding?

- Why did the loon get a present?

Example stories from children

Bruce's snake story

Snake slithers all around the colours. He finds the red by a fire. The orange by a tree. The yellow by the sun. Green: grass. Blue: water. Purple – that's tricky.

I want some blue and some purple and some yellow. I'm making a pattern. That's better. Look at all the colours.

Purple stick man comes along. 'Where did you get those colours?' he asks. 'I got my purple self from a little tree branch.'

'Can I have some of your purple?' asks snake.

'You've already got some of that. Can you give me some colours? I want to look pretty like you.'

'Do you want red?' asks the snake.

'No, it gets me too hot.'

'Yellow?'

'No, it gets me too hot.'

'Green?'

'Yes, I want some of that. There we are. I like that.'

'But I think it needs a bit more at the top. Can I have some blue? That's better.'

They keep their beautiful patterns for ever and ever.

Follow-up activities

A necklace for the loon (suitable for 3yrs+ only): thread large beads, or big pasta tubes dyed with food colouring, to make a necklace. (**Safety:** make sure children are supervised, especially younger children as the beads might be a choking hazard). Make a collection of all your favourite colours: or restrict the colours to two or three, to make an alternating pattern. Ask children to copy and continue an adult's pattern, and then invite them to make up their own pattern.

Colour collection: collect a range of objects in bright colours: blocks, crayons, small toys, etc. Invite children to make patterns by arranging them on big sheets of paper. Take photos of the results.

Lily made a pattern on a piece of paper using a collection of round counters. She filled the paper carefully, spacing the counters out regularly and evenly. I commented that it looked a bit like the endpapers of 'The Very Hungry Caterpillar'. Lily found a little toy caterpillar and positioned it in the corner next to one of the circles. 'Look,' she said 'He's eaten all those holes in the food.'

Marbling patterns: these are exciting for children to explore. Use marbling inks in a tray of water, and watch how the ink forms swirls and spirals as the children mix it in the water.

Felting: this also offers a multi-sensory way to explore the patterns colours can make when they are felted together.

Bird song patterns: use two contrasting instruments to represent two birds, or use 'singing' bird toys. Make them have a conversation with each other, alternating the two voices. Talk about the pattern you have made.

Circle games

- **Pass the drum:** ask children to pass a small drum silently round the circle. Sing or chant a rhyme, for instance:

  Pass the drum from me to you, to you
  Pass the drum and do just what I do.

  At the end of the rhyme, the person holding the drum taps a simple pattern and everybody claps the rhythm they made.

Daily routines

- Clapping patterns are a great way to get a group of children listening and paying attention: try tapping the rhythms of different tunes: different body percussion patterns – e.g. clap your hands then slap your knees: or voice patterns, e.g. 'Aha, oho, aha, oho' etc.

Outdoor activities

- **Where did the colours fall?** Cut up a paint sample sheet to make lots of small squares of many different shades. Put them in a box. Explain that you've caught some of specks of the rainbow snake's colours. Give each child a colour and ask them to find something of the exact same colour somewhere outside.

- **Look at pictures of patterned animals** – particularly close-ups of fur, feather, and scales – and paint your own patterned pictures in response. For example, Jiarui looked at the markings on a toy owl and said: *'It's an owl, but it's got a tiger on it!'*.

- **Invite children to choose an animal with camouflage markings** – a toy or a picture – and hide it in a place where it can't be spotted.

- **Follow my leader:** how did the birds travel as they went on their search? See if you can copy their ways of moving in different patterns, following a leader: walk, walk, jump jump, zigzag and then straight, stretching high and bending low.

Using ICT

- Inclusive Technology's 'Kaleidoscope' offers a way of making and observing changing patterns (www.inclusive.co.uk/k-1-p2296).

- Make patterned pictures on a touchscreen computer using a programme like 'Revelation art' that offers stamps and shapes (see Further resources).

- Of the many games matching colours to make a pattern, Crickweb's Early Years – Train game is one that children enjoy: http://www.crickweb.co.uk/Early-Years.html

- There are many online versions of the 'pocket Simon' game that challenges children to make and copy tunes, e.g. Chimes from Primary resources: http://www.primaryresources.co.uk/online/Chimes.html

- Listen to some common bird songs (for instance on this website: http://www.british-birdsongs.uk/). See if the children can copy the different sounds, as in the 'singing bird' game above.

Younger children

- Very young children love tapping and banging: particularly on resonant surfaces like metal trays or cake tins. You may be surprised by how rhythmically they play! If an adult joins in with them, they will often spontaneously take turns, making a pattern of 'you play, I play'.

The awareness of colour and pattern begins very young. *Example: Baby Evie enjoyed playing with a colourful collection of feathers: picking them up and dropping them, or trying to catch them when they are blown in the air with a balloon pump. She explored scraps of coloured wrapping paper, different colours and shapes. Outdoors she looked intently at the patterns that leaves and branches make against the sky.*

Footprints in the sand

Mark-making and recording

- **Pattern hunt:** look for different patterns in the environment around you, both indoors and out: zig-zag, wiggly, stripy, dotty. Fold a long thin piece of paper in 4 to make a snake-shaped zig-zag book, and fill each page with a different pencil pattern.

Assessment opportunities

Children's mark-making doesn't need to use pens or paintbrushes. Free pattern-making with objects give a real insight into children's engagement with patterns. For example, in the story we arranged lolly sticks on a white snake-shaped piece of cloth to make coloured patterns. Extend the activity by using 2D shapes – buttons or even sugar cubes.

James was playing with a collection of foot cutouts. He arranged them in a regular pattern, red, blue, red, blue. 'Don't walk on these! I haven't finished yet. I'm going to get all the way over there. Red blue blue – that's wrong. Now I've got it right. I've made a path. You can use it to go somewhere now.'

Chloe spent a long time arranging sugar cubes in a row. Then she started to make another row on top. 'It's a wall. I need more bricks. It's for little people to climb. When I got up to 20 then I ran out of bricks. I had to get some more.

What to look for

Do children spontaneously place objects to make patterns? Can they copy repeating patterns? Can they make their own patterns? Can they join in with patterns of body percussion?

Songs

All songs involve rhythm and pattern: children are learning about patterns of sound every time they clap along to the tune of a familiar rhyme.

For a song to relate to the story, try 'I can sing a rainbow' with this:

'I can sing a rainbow'
*Red and yellow and pink and green
Purple and orange and blue,
I can sing a rainbow,
Sing a rainbow,
Sing a rainbow too.*

*Listen with your ears,
Listen with your eyes,
And sing everything you see!
I can sing a rainbow,
Sing a rainbow,
Sing along with me...*

Let children wave coloured scarves to this well-known song.

(Source: Arthur Hamilton, 1955. www.bbc.co.uk/schoolradio/ subjects/earlylearning/nurserysongs/F-J/sing_a_rainbow)

Sung to the tune of 'Bobby Shaftoe', 'Clap your hands' invites children to make up their own patterns for subsequent verses:

Clap your hands
*Clap your hands and wiggle your fingers
Clap your hands and wiggle your fingers
Clap your hands and wiggle your fingers
Now you've made a pattern*

(Source: Nicholls, S. (1992) *Bobby Shaftoe Clap Your Hands*)

Additional stories

- Sharratt, N. (2012) *My Mum and Dad make me Laugh*

- Zolotow, C. and Sendak, M. (2002) *Mr. Rabbit and the lovely Present*

- A version of the story based on the colourful book by Joanna Troughton, *How the Birds Changed their Feathers*, is on YouTube here: https://www.youtube.com/watch?v=Xbg0h8KurLk

Links to other parts of the book

This module fits well with:

✓ Number 2: symmetry, counting in 2s

✓ Number 4: 2D shape

✓ Number 10: counting in 10s

Number Ten – Counting

EYFS Maths Objectives

✓ Show curiosity about numbers by offering comments or asking questions (Number 30-50 mths).

✓ Count reliably with numbers from one to 20, place them in order and say which number is one more or one less than a given number (Number early learning goal).

✓ Recognise some numerals of particular interest (Number 40-60 mths).

Resources

A wipeable hundred square and whiteboard pens. Two dolls: a princess doll and a Jack doll. A selection of very small natural objects, for example, some leftover pot-pourri, small stones and shells.

Once upon a number: 10

Recognising the number ten, and understanding that one number can be made up of two digits, is an important step forward for children, dramatically expanding their ability to count.

Ten, and learning the trick of counting in tens, is important in helping children to understand the patterns of numbers in a hundred square. In the story, they learn to move up and down the hundred square as well as along and

The Magic Forest

This story harnesses children's interest and excitement about big numbers, and enables them to explore a hundred square in an open-ended way. This is a classic Grimm's tale about a hero who uses his own resources to overcome an insuperable task. And this applies to the mathematics behind the story too.

Story outline: The Magic Forest

Jack lived on the edge of the forest of magic numbers. The forest was full of strange plants and creatures. At the other end of the forest lived the beautiful princess. Jack wanted to go and see the princess, but it was hard to walk through the forest. He could only go forwards and back on the roads through the trees, or up and down the paths of numbers.

He set off along the squares, counting all the way: 1, 2, 3, 4, 5, 6: but then he had to stop, because in the path ahead of him was a poisonous flower. He had to turn and go down the path of 6's: 6, 16, 26, 36,... But on the path of 6's he heard a buzzing noise. It was a bee. *'Help Jack, I'm in trouble. I've been squashed and stomped on by*

a magician.' So Jack straightened out the bee's legs and smoothed down her wings. *'Thank you, Jack, I'll help you sometime.'*

So Jack went on through the forest until he got to the magician's castle. He wanted to marry the princess. *'I can't marry anyone, Jack, until I find my pot of magic honey.'*

Jack went to ask the bee for help. *'The honey is in the forest of numbers. It's at number 72.'* So Jack looked under all the rocks and plants in the forest of magic numbers until he found number 72. He took the honey to the princess and they lived happily ever after.

Story summary

Jack journeys through the magic forest to find the princess.

He helps some creatures in the forest.

They help him finish some magical tasks so that he can marry the princess.

back, laying the groundwork for learning how to add on tens and how to work with 2-digit numbers. The story uses a 1-100 square. You may want also to show children a 0-99 hundred square, where the tens are in a different position.

Why this story?

A hundred seems an impossibly large number to a child who can barely count to 10. Perhaps for this reason, many children are fascinated by hundred squares. But although understanding how these numbers work may seem an impossible task to a young child, they find out that the techniques they have learnt for dealing with smaller numbers work here too. The number 10 does its organising magic, ensuring that all the 6s and all the 2s line up in rows. Counting along from 32 to 37 is no different from counting along from 2 to 7.

Children with grid schemas cluster round these kinds of activities and think of many ways to investigate and play with a 100-square. Even children with no understanding of numerals enjoy taking part in the story. As they follow the hero's progress along the number board they begin to develop concepts of 'few' and 'many', 'close' and 'far'. Children find the story of the journey through the forest gripping and can recall it weeks later. Rose, for instance, saw a 100 square on the computer screen and said *'That's just like the story you told us, the one with the poisonous flower.'* The excitement of the story reflects the excitement mathematicians feel in exploring the world of numbers.

Joining in with the story

Before you start the story, encourage the children to look at the 100 square and say what they notice.

'I like 100,' said Lilian. *'No, I like 72. Because if you add 100 and 72 together, you get a very big number.'* Jairui surprised us by how many numbers he recognised, and the way he spotted patterns on the number square: *'There's 60. 60, 70, 80, 90. There's 100. Look, 1, zero zero. It's the biggest number.'*

Theo could only recognise one number, but it still allowed him to make discoveries about the hundred square. 'I like 3,' he said, *'Because I'm 3. I can find another 3. Look, there's two 3s together. A 3 and another one.'*

Get the children to practise moving Jack along the board from 1-10, saying the numbers as Jack lands on each square. Then ask them to move him backwards, again saying the numbers. What about if he goes up or down the columns of numbers? For example, Caitlin said, *'He's got to go down, that way'*, pointing, *'With all the sixes.'*

Allow the children to help arrange some of the resources to become challenges or dangers in the forest on some of the squares, naming the number on the square they choose. Many of the ideas in the story above, for example, came from children in one particular group: *'That's Jack's house. He's on number 1.'* *'That's a poisonous flower. That's another one. It's going next to the other one. It's on number 7. This one's going right in the middle.'*

In the original Grimm folktale, Jack helps a bee, a duck and an ant, who then help him collect grains of wheat from a field, retrieve a ring from the bottom of a pond, and find the honey; but the children can suggest what creatures are trapped in the forest, and what their problem is. (For example, 'The bee's hurt,' they told me. 'The magician squashed him. He just stamped on him.')

They can decide on the task that the princess sets Jack – the number of tasks can be varied according to the children's age and attention.

Big questions

- Which number do you like? Can you find more of that number?

- Can you see a square with two numerals on it? Can you find two numerals the same on one square?

- Can you find a number with a zero at the end?

- Which is the biggest number? Which is the smallest?

- Why do you think Jack wants to see the princess? Is it going to be easy to find her? The road ahead of him is blocked: which way will he go now? Jack has to find the princess' honey: who could he ask for help?

- Do you think Jack married the princess? Where do you think they lived – Jack's house or the princess'?

- Can you find the square with the bee on it? What numbers does it have on it?

Example stories from children

Rose and Florence's story

Rose told a story using the 100 square on the interactive whiteboard.

She used a puppet to 'walk' along the numbers: 'Jack's walking through the forest. He started on 1, 2, 3, 4, 5, 6, 7, Stop! Because there's a scary thing.'

He's got to go a different way. Down past all the sevens. Because of my dangerous flower. He got in another dangerous place because of a scary witch. I'm using Jack to be my finger. He's getting to 100. I like zero.'

Florence: I like zero too. Because with zero and one you can make ten! I'm drawing a monster. His eyes are zeros. Jack has to fight him.

Follow-up activities

Jack and the princess leave the palace and set off for more adventures. The children can move Jack through the forest:

'He can't go that way. He has to go round. He's got to go down and then backwards, 5, 4, 3…'.

What do they notice about the numbers? Can they move him all around the edge of the board? Try a different way of moving: what about moving diagonally? What do they notice if they move diagonally from 11?

Counting the numbers out loud as the children move along the squares. Stop when you get to ten and discuss what the next number should be and how you get there. See if the children can join in counting all the way to 100.

Cover up some of the squares with shells or stones: ask children to guess what number is hidden under the shell. What strategies do they use to work it out? Let them cover up numbers for their friends to guess.

Put one shell or bead on every square, covering up the numbers. Can you still count to 100?

Playdough snakes: challenge the children to make playdough 'snakes' to join two numbers: which snake will be longer, one going from 2-8, or one going from 2-12? You could add in lolly sticks to make a game of snakes and ladders.

Can the children build a castle for the princess? She has exactly 10 bricks in each wall. Can they make a palace with 10 walls?

The princess loves jewels. If possible, invest in some sets of Indian bracelets and some dishes or a bracelet tree. Ask the children to sort them into piles of 10.

Draw a 100 grid on a large piece of paper or card. Offer the children a variety of tiny things. Challenge them to see if they can stick one object in each box.

Make a 100 square grid on transparent paper – for instance a printable overhead projector sheet. Put it over a page of a book with detailed pictures: eg *Where's Wally?* or *You Choose*. Ask the children to play I-Spy, following challenges and making up their own: 'Can you see what's on square 72?'. 'Which square has a cat on it?'

Circle games

- **Play a game of hide and seek:** encourage the 'seeker' to count in tens. The people hiding will soon realise that they have to hide very quickly!

draw some doors on the walls and label them with two or three digit numbers. Make envelopes with corresponding numbers on them. Ask children to deliver the pretend letters to the right house.

Using ICT

- Download a picture of a 100 square into a favourite drawing programme on a touch screen. Challenge the children to colour in all the number 5s, or all the zeroes. What patterns do they notice?

- Project an image of a hundred square on a blank wall. Can the children make their shadow fingers touch a particular number?

- Make a 100 square grid for a Beebot™ or programmable toy to move along. The children could use two digit number cards to set each other challenges: can you find this number on the board and get Beebot™ there?

For younger children

- Young children often love collections of tiny objects: sorting through a pile of gravel, playing with beans and seeds, or picking up tiny sequins. Some settings provide a 'miniature table' or a 'finger gym' where the children are offered, for instance, small bottles, little spoons and grains of coloured rice. It helps their fine motor coordination, so helpful for counting, and their experience of 'many'.

  Safety: if there is a risk of children putting small objects in their mouths, try offering them edible treasures. For instance, baby Evie spent a long time picking up and eating blueberries one by one.

- To understand the 'ten-ness' of ten, **sing songs** like '10 in a bed' using ten children under a blanket, or '10 green bottles' using ten plastic bottles.

Daily routines

Time is another area of mathematics where children encounter big numbers. Those little marks round the edge of a clock are interesting to children in the same way as the numbers of a hundred square. Can children manage to stay quiet for a whole minute? Can they watch as the second hand goes all the way round the clock? Can they wait for a minute with their eyes shut and open it when the minute is up?

Outdoor activities

- Try retelling the story in a woodland setting. Bring back natural resources to recreate the story: or ask the children to map the story by drawing their adventures on a 100-square. There are always plenty of opportunities to count large numbers of objects outside. (For example, on a trip to the forest, Lily was disappointed. 'This isn't a forest,' she said, 'It's only a wood. There aren't enough trees for it to be a forest.' I told her that it's a forest if there are too many trees to count. But Lily was too clever for me. 'I'm not going to count them, because I know it's a wood.')

- Explore big numbers in a playground or garden. With chalk,

Footprints in the sand

Mark-making

Pages with numbers on – calendars, raffle tickets, numbered lists – encourage children to make numerical marks.

James found a page of an old calendar. He used it to invent his own game of snakes and ladders. He talked as he drew his game.

'You've got to follow the arrows. What do the arrows say? You have to go up this ladder here. Oh-oh. Do not land on 4! That's a ladder, a really tall ladder, but when you get up there, there's this horrible snake that takes you all the way down to 1.'

Let children draw on a whiteboard hundred square with wipeable pens. Let them invent imaginary journeys, and talk to you about where they are going.

Assessment Opportunities

Find practical tasks which will encourage children to keep tallies and make marks. Sort out a box of toys with the children, asking them to work out how many there are. Or count up the proceeds of a sale or the cash till of a play shop by piling the coins in 10s.

Offer writing materials, to see how they use marks to record their counting. Suggest sorting the objects into piles of 10, or model how to keep tallies by making a mark for each object.

What to look for

Do children show an interest in large numbers? Do they spot patterns, ask questions, think of problems? Can they count and order numbers with 1:1 correspondence? Do they recognise 1- and 2-digit numbers?

Songs

Some well known counting songs:

10 in the bed
There were 10 in the bed and the little one said,
'Roll over, roll over.'

So they all rolled over and one fell out,

There were 9 in the bed….

(Source: traditional: Dale, P. (2013) Ten in the Bed)

10 Green bottles
10 green bottles, hanging on the wall
10 green bottles, hanging on the wall
But if 1 green bottle should accidentally fall,
there'd be 9 green bottles, hanging on the wall….

(Source: traditional, Matterson, E. *This Little Puffin*)

A good song to introduce the story:

- Walking through the Jungle' watch it here: https://www.youtube.com/watch?v=VE4fC0Sdl60

(or use the book by Julie Lacome (1995) *Walking Through the Jungle.*)

Additional stories

The text of the original story is on this website: http://www.gutenberg.org/files/2591/2591-h/2591-h.htm#link2H_4_0040 or in: Pullman, P. (2013) *Grimm Tales*.

Other stories about walking through a forest:

- Berkes, M. (2007) *Over in the Jungle*

- Browne, A. (2010) *Bear Hunt*

Books with big numbers in:

- Goodhart, P. and Sharratt, N. (2004) *You Choose*

- Handford, M. (2007) *Where's Wally?*

- Niemenen L. (2013) *Walk this World*

- Sayre, A.P. and J. (2003) *One is a Snail*

Links to other parts of the book

This module fits well with:

✓ Number 3: position and direction

✓ Number 11: counting out

Number Eleven – Estimation

EYFS Maths Objectives

✓ Select a small number of objects from a group (Number 22-36 mths).

✓ Count out up to six objects from a larger group (Number 40-60 mths).

✓ Use some language of quantities, such as 'more' and 'a lot' (Number 22-36 mths).

✓ Estimate how many objects they can see and check by counting them (Number 40-60 mths).

✓ Using quantities and objects, add and subtract two single-digit numbers (Number early learning goal).

Resources

The story could be told on a small scale, with small ornamental pebbles piled into two mountains, and small figures for the old man and the Laughing Buddha, or outdoors, with a collection of large beach pebbles.

story for children too, with the message that small children can, like the children in the story, achieve big things as a group.

The story explores the power of larger numbers and allows children to practise estimation skills, and counting out small numbers of objects.

The Old Man and the Mountains

This folktale is a political fable from China. In the past, the mountain to be moved represented a corrupt government. It's an important

Once upon a number: 11

Children can count ten objects on their ten fingers: but once they reach 11, they enter a realm of abstraction where they

Story outline: The Old Man and the Mountains

A long time ago there were two great mountains: Taihan mountain and Wangwu mountain. An old man lived in a village at the bottom of the mountains, and he didn't like it one bit. The mountains blocked the sun from his village. When he wanted to take his rice down the Han river to sell at the market, he had to travel all the way round the mountains to get there.

One day he decided *'I am going to move those troublesome mountains and put them in the sea.'*

So every time he went to the market, he picked up a stone from the mountain, carried it with him and threw it in the sea.

At the bend in the river lived the Laughing Buddha. He watched the old man, and one day he asked him: *'What are you doing?'*

The old man explained, and the Buddha laughed and laughed.

'You foolish old man' he said. *'You can never move a whole mountain by yourself!'*

Maybe I can't do it myself,' said the old man. *'But I have children and grand-children and great-grand-children, who will carry on the task after I am gone. A mountain has no children. One day they will be mightier than the mountain.'*

The next day he called his family. *'Sons, daughters, come and help me! 'Grandchildren and great-grandchildren, come and help me! Help me throw the mountains in the sea.'*

'We'll help you, dad!' 'We'll help you, granddad!' they answered.

Each of his family picked up one rock, and carried it down the river towards the sea.

Laughing Buddha was worried. *'Maybe the old man is right,'* he said. *Perhaps he really will destroy the mountains.'*

So he called for his two dragon friends. They each picked up one mountain, put them on their backs, and moved them to the other side of the river, where they still are to this very day.

Story summary

An old man decides to move the mountains that are blocking his road. He picks up one rock at a time and takes it to the sea.

The Buddha laughs at him, but he explains that his family and all his descendants will be stronger than the mountains and one day be able to move them

When Buddha sees all the old man's family helping him, he is worried, so he sends his dragon friends to move the mountains out of the old man's way.

can't depend on fingers so easily. Understanding number 11 is a real step forward in mathematical learning.

Children readily learn to recite numbers to 10. When they realise how, in our culture, with number 11, the digits repeat themselves and we start again from one, they begin to understand that counting can go on for ever. This story needs lots of objects, and 11 symbolises a number bigger than you can readily count.

Why this story?

Another 'transporting' story, this one draws on children's fascination with stones, and piles of objects: and the idea that even tiny objects, added together, can make something enormous. The stones that make up the mountain become too many to be counted, giving a chance to introduce estimation skills.

Joining in with the story

Before the story starts, you can ask the children to find a stone each and pile them up to make the mountains (if they are put on a cloth or a dish, they are easier to carry away at the end). Encourage the children to take on the role of the children in the story by asking them, 'Will you help me?'. Ask some of them to take the stones, one at a time, from the mountains and put them in the sea. Watch how the mountains shrink and how the pile in the sea grows.

Big questions

- The old man isn't happy. What could he do? Will you help the old man?

- Can you pick up one stone? Two stones? Can you pick up six stones?

● How many rocks do you think there are in the sea? Are there more in the sea or more on the mountain? Do you think the old man will manage to move the whole mountain? Why did Buddha laugh?

● Do you think you could move a whole mountain?

Example stories from children

Amelia and Sam were interested in the basket of stones, and took turns filling it up. Their discussion shows clearly the conflict between their counting ability and their physical coordination.

Sam and Amelia's story

Sam: I'm going to put 3 in.

Amelia: I'll tell you when to stop.

(Sam puts 2 stones in slowly: Amelia counts too quickly for him): '1,2,3, stop!'

Amelia: That's wrong. We need more.

Sam: We need 3. He holds up 3 fingers.

Amelia: No, we need 1,2…

Sam: 3! 1 more. No, 3. (He puts in 2 more.)

Amelia: There's too many.

Sam: But I need this many! (He holds up 5 fingers. He takes all the stones out and starts again. He puts in 4 stones.) No, I need this many! (He holds up 5 fingers and then puts the thumb down.) This many!

Amelia: These can be the eggs.

Sam: The dragon's coming through. Here we come: he can carry the box. Oops...

Amelia: We broke it. The dragon broke the box.

Follow-up activities

Counting out: ask children to take one, then two stones and drop them in the 'sea'. Then ask if anyone is strong enough to take more than 2: ask them to count 5 or 6 stones into a hand or a pot before adding them to the pile in the sea. Finally count all the stones at the end! Counting out is harder than counting a group of objects, so work with relatively small numbers.

Many children find it hard to stop counting when they are

counting out. Model how to do this with a 'silly' dragon puppet, who can't count out correctly. Decide how many stones the dragon is going to pick up. Ask the children to hold up the right number as a reminder. As the puppet begins counting, ask the children to shout out 'stop' when he gets to the right number.

Moving and counting: there are many mathematical possibilities in simply moving the stones from the mountains to the sea. It gives children practice in moving objects as they count. It allows children to estimate which of two collections has more. Because one set of stones is piled up and the other is spread out, the children can see how the same number of objects will look different depending on how they are arranged.

Estimation game: the dragon has got a bagful of stones to move, but he doesn't know how many. He is going to 'estimate' or 'guess'. Make sure the dragon guesses a number that is close but not accurate. Then count the stones to check. Briefly show the children a bowl or see-through bag with a different number of stones – about 8 or 9 – and ask them to guess the number, by showing with their fingers how many they think are. Children often are reluctant to estimate a number, because they want to be exactly right. Explain that, when you are estimating, being close is as important as being right. Repeat the activity with different numbers of objects. You could ask the children to record their guesses on paper or whiteboards, or by choosing a number card.

The treasure dice game: a game for a pair of children. Each child needs a basket with five pretend sweets or jewels in.

The children take turns to throw a die numbered 1-3, and count out the right number of sweets to give their friend. The game lasts until one child has all the sweets (which can take a long time!). Extend the game by using ten sweets and a 1-6 die.

James and George are at different stages of learning to count, but both of them got very involved in this game.

To begin with George looked carefully at the spots on the dice. 'I've got 3 on mine,' he said. He turned it round: 'Now I've only got 2.'

He threw the dice and carefully put three 'jewels' in James' basket. James was delighted. 'I've got all these!' he said.

George looked in his own basket. 'That's not many – it's only 4.'

After a while, James got interested in seeing how many jewels he could cram into his basket. When it came to tidying up, he put every single jewel in his own basket and then emptied them carefully into the box.

Circle games

11 Steps: stand in a circle. Everyone takes 11 steps towards the middle (or 5, or 7), counting out loud all together. Then take the same number of steps back again. Then repeat, but this time pretend you are walking on jelly, or tiptoeing on ice. Imagine there is a mound of ice-cream in the middle of the circle, or a scary dragon. (If you prefer, sing the numbers, as in the song 'Seven steps' from supersimplelearning.com/songs/original-series/one/seven-steps/).

Daily routines

Birthdays are a great opportunity for enjoyable mathematics. You can make a big performance of getting out the right number of candles, counting out the right number with the children and asking: *'how many have I lit now? How many still to go?'* Children are very motivated to make sure there are the right number of candles.

Laying the table involves children in counting out the right quantities: can they find four spoons, or three plates?

Outdoor activities

- Get a large bag of seaside stones from a garden centre. Ask the children to move the pile from one area to another, using barrows, baskets and trolleys. Ask them to guess or count how many stones they have moved.

- Teaching children to stop is a good thing to do outside. Ask a child to run about and stop on a signal. Show them how to plant both their feet on the ground, saying '1, 2!' as each foot hits the ground. It will help their physical coordination and their counting too.

Using ICT

Simple computer games and apps like 'Feed the Monkey' from Busythings (a free app from: itunes.apple.com/us/app/feed-the-monkey/id600524229?mt=8) require children to count out the right number of objects, with a self-checking reward.

Younger children

Young children love to explore big collections of objects: a ball pool full of balls, or a big tower of bricks to knock down. Babies, too, enjoy practising the hardest part of counting – how to stop.

Example: Baby Evie likes to hold her mum's hands and clap them together. Her mum joins in with Evie's rhythm and says 'clap, clap, clap, stop!' Evie laughs when the clapping stops.

Footprints in the sand

Mark-making

Play a game seeing who can throw balls in a bucket, or bean bags in a hoop. Ask children to record on a clipboard how

many times their friend scored. Let them find their own ways of recording this first, and then, if appropriate, show them how to make a tally chart. Invite them to find other things to tally: children in the setting, windows in the building, bikes in the bike shed.

Assessment opportunities

Offer free play with collections of objects: for instance a bag of buttons and little test tubes or jars to count them into: beads and tweezers to pick them up with; small shells in the water tray and nets. Observe children's spontaneous mathematical behaviour, or set them small challenges.

Safety: make sure younger children are not offered objects which might be a choking hazard, and supervise where necessary.

What to look for

What strategies do children use to count out? Do they count accurately? Do they remember to stop counting? Do they count spontaneously, or only when prompted by an adult? Can they make realistic estimates of a small number of objects?

- Hayes, S. (1992) *Nine Ducks Nine*

- Fromental, J-L., Jolivet, J. (2007) *365 Penguins*

Songs

Build a house
Build a house with five bricks
One, two, three, four, five
Put a roof on top
And a chimney, too
Where the wind blows through...
WHOO WHOO!

(Source: Matteson, E. *This Little Puffin*)

One potato
One potato, two potato, three potato, four!
Five potato, six potato, seven potato, more!

(Source: Matteson, E. *This Little Puffin*)

Additional stories

- An original text of the story is available on:
  www.chinavista.com/experience/story/story3.html

Other stories with plenty of things to count:

- Andreae, G. and Sharratt, N. (2003) *Pants*

- Blake, Q. (1994) *Cockatoos*

Links to other parts of the book

This module fits well with:

✓ Chapter 10: counting large numbers

✓ Chapter 12: estimation and capacity

Number Twelve – Capacity

EYFS Maths Objectives

✓ Fill and empty containers (Shape, space and measure, 16-26 months).

✓ Use shapes appropriately for tasks (Shape, space and measure, 30-50 months).

✓ Order two items by weight or capacity (Shape, space and measure, 40-60months).

✓ Use everyday language to talk about capacity and compare quantities (Shape, space and measure, early learning goal).

Resources

Two animal figures, a cat and a mouse, a collection of conkers, and different size containers in a variety of shapes and materials.

The Cat, the Mouse and the Conkers

The excitement of collecting conkers lends itself to a story about capacity: comparing sizes, weighing, filling and emptying, more and less. The simple conker encourages mathematical language from children and the story uses children's ideas about the games they like to play with conkers.

Once upon a number: 12

A round dozen, 12 is a good number for collections. 12 conkers is enough to fill a large egg box or a small tin.

It can be divided in half and in half again, perfect for introducing the vocabulary of capacity: half-full, just a few, nearly all gone.

Story outline: The Cat, the Mouse and the Conkers

A cat and a mouse once became friends. Every day they played in the park together. One day they found some conkers under a horse chestnut tree.

'Let's play with them!' said the cat.

'We must keep these to eat in the winter,' said the sensible mouse. So she got out her useful tin. She put in enough conkers to cover the bottom of the tin.

'We need some more,' said the mouse. So they put in more conkers until the tin was half full.

'We still need some more,' said the mouse. They carried on putting in more conkers until the tin was full.

'We need to keep these conkers somewhere safe,' said the mouse. They went down the road, across the churchyard, opened the heavy wooden door of the church, and put the conkers in the big iron chest at the back of the church.

The next day, the cat asked: *'Shall we get the conkers from the chest in the church and play with them?'*

'No,' said the mouse, *'We're saving them until winter comes.'*

But the cat really wanted to play with the conkers. She said to the mouse, *'I have to go out this afternoon. I've been invited to my cat friend's birthday party.'*

But she did not go to a birthday party. She went down the road, across the churchyard, through the wooden door, opened the chest at the back of the church and took out the top layer of conkers from the tin. She played at rolling them across the church floor until they all rolled away into cracks and down holes and disappeared.

When she got back home, the mouse wanted to know all about it: *'Did you have a good time at your friend's party? What did you play? What's your friend called?'*

The cat said: *'My friend is called 'Top-off!' and we played rolling and hiding in holes.'*

The next day, the cat wanted to play with the conkers again. Again she pretended she was going to a party. But really she went down the road, across the churchyard, through the wooden door, opened the chest at the back of the church and took out half the conkers from the tin.

She played hide and seek with them in the long grass of the churchyard until they were lost. When she got back home, the mouse asked: *'What was your friend called?'*

'Half-gone,' said the cat.

The third day, the cat set off to another birthday party.

'What a lot of parties! Can I come too?' asked the mouse.

'You wouldn't enjoy it,' said the cat.

The cat went down the road to the church and took out all the conkers. She played jumping on the conkers until they were all broken. When she got home, the mouse asked: *'What was your friend's name?'*

'All-gone,' said the cat.

'Top-off, half-gone, all-gone: those are funny names,' said the mouse. She began to feel worried about the conkers. So the mouse went down the road to the church and looked in the tin. When she came back, she was very angry with the cat.

But the cat just snarled. She opened her mouth and showed the mouse her sharp white teeth. The mouse ran away and never played with cats again.

Story summary

The cat and the mouse collect conkers in a tin – just a few, half full, quite full. They hide it in a safe place.

Each day the cat pretends she is going to a birthday party, but really she goes and plays with the conkers until they are all gone.

She tells the mouse her birthday friends are called 'top-off, half-gone, all-gone.' The mouse checks on the conkers and finds the cat has tricked her.

Why this story?

This story is about wanting 'more', an important word for very young children, especially ones who like collecting. An adaptation of an old folktale, it taps into the excitement of finding and hoarding conkers, lying like jewels in the grass, yet dull and lifeless within a couple of days.

It has a different way of introducing vocabulary connected with capacity in the shape of cats called 'Top-off' 'Half-gone' and 'All-gone'.

Joining in with the story

Let the children help choose which tin to fill – if you have enough tins and conkers each child can fill their own – and experiment with putting different amounts of conkers in. Ask them to describe how full their container is, modelling the language of capacity if necessary: 'just a few' 'nearly full' 'practically empty': what does it look like to have a tin that's 'half-gone'?

There are many points in the story where you can incorporate children's suggestions, e.g. 'I pick up conkers on the green outside my house,' said one child. In the original story, the cat and mouse hide the conkers in the church strong box – the traditional place for people to keep their valuables. But children will have their own ideas about a place that is very safe. (For example, James was full of ideas of games to play with conkers: his suggestions are in the story.)

Big questions

- Is it a good idea or a bad idea for a mouse to make friends with a cat? What games might they play together? What do you like to play with conkers?

- Which would be the best container for the mouse to keep conkers in? Can you fill the tin half0full? Fill it up?

- Where would be a safe place to keep the conkers near here? How do you get there? Do you think the cat is really going to a birthday party, or is she tricking the mouse? Do you think a mouse should go to a cat's birthday party?

- How did the mouse feel when she saw the empty tin? What did she say to the cat?

Example stories from children

Mabel, like the mouse, was very keen on collecting the conkers. Once she had got a bagful she absolutely did not want to take any out again, but kept a firm grip on the the bag.

Mabel's story

'The mouse is picking up conkers. This one [the mouse] only does one [at a time], doesn't it? (Mabel makes the mouse put conkers one at a time into the box. She wants a bag to put them in. (She collects a bagful and pours it into the box.) The mouse has got all the conkers. She's keeping them in the box. You can't have any. You can look. You can put one more in. Not two, just one. Now you can put another in. That's all.'

James, like the cat, enjoyed rolling, throwing and experimenting with the conkers: he put them in a box, emptied them out, lined them up and counted them. His stories were much more wide-ranging:

James' story

'What if there was a cat chasing a mouse, and a dog chasing the cat? What then?

I think there would be only a dog left.

But what if the mouse hid in a hole under a rock in India?'

Follow-up activities

Ask children to collect conkers and put them in a big sand tray or tub. To begin with, just the conkers on their own can be fun to play with; then add in tins, boxes, lids, paper bags, bowls. Make sure there are different sizes and materials. Extend the play further with pipes, puppets, leaves, or wooden numerals. Set some of the following challenges. Try pouring conkers from a wide flat tin to a tall thin tin. Which one holds more? Roll conkers down a tube or pipe. Can the children catch the conkers in a tin at the bottom?

Estimating: drop conkers into a tin one at a time. Can the children count the sounds as the conkers hit the tin? Can they guess in advance how many conkers it will take to fill the tin?

The previous chapter suggested games for encouraging children to estimate numbers. Use the same strategies when asking them to estimate capacity. Ask children to guess how many conkers they will be able to pick up in one handful. Let them try, and see if they are right. Guess how many handfuls it will take to fill a tin/half fill a tin. Pour that tin into a bigger tin. Guess how full the big tin will be when the small tin is emptied into it. How many tinfuls will it take to fill the big tin?

Other role play scenarios: cat has a tummy ache and mouse is going to make some magic medicine to make him feel better. Offer the children small bottles, drippers, spoons, glitter, coloured water to make medicine. Or outside, show them how to grind leaves in a pestle and mortar to add colour and smell to the liquid. **Health and safety:** remind children that this is only pretend medicine: use it as an opportunity for talking about when and why to take medicine in real life. Or if you prefer, mouse could make a magic potion to make cat fly/turn her into a frog/stop her being greedy.

Sell bags and pots of conkers in a conker shop. Introduce a scale so that the children can weigh their conkers: does this bag weigh more than that tin?

Circle games

Fireman's chain: give each child a bucket and ask them to stand in a long line. Pour water into the first child's bucket and ask them to pass the water down the line, from one bucket to the next. How much water is left at the end?

Daily routines

- When pouring drinks, ask the children how much they would like in their glass, encouraging them to use words like: full, empty, half-full.

- **Tidying up:** when the floor is a sea of toys, give children a basket and see whether they can fill it with one particular item: all the Lego®, all the crayons etc. Who can be the first to fill their basket?

Outdoor activities

- **The handful challenge:** scatter a bag of conkers over the grass. See how many conkers children can pick up using just one hand/crawling only. Give each child a pot or tin. How full can you fill your tin before the timer runs out? Or hide the conkers under a rug: children have to feel under the rug to collect their conkers.

- **Mud kitchen:** use conkers as a 'cooking' ingredient outside. Add in shallow pans and tall jugs, cooking utensils, egg boxes.

- Hide conkers in sand and provide sieves and spades to help get them out.

- Put out a rain gauge or a jar with straight see-through sides. Every day, inspect how much water is left in, and make a mark on the side to show where the water has got to. How many days before the jar is full?

Using ICT

- Introduce children to the 'fill' tool. '2draw', from 2simple, has an easy option which allows children to make shapes and then fill them with different colours: Or 'Tizzy's Busy Week' from Sherston Software offers a game decorating Tizzy's bathroom where children click on shapes to fill them with colour. (See Further resources for more information.)

- Poisson Rouge's 'Collecting pollen' game is also about filling and emptying: www.poissonrouge.com/android/bugs.html

- Crick Web's simple game, 'Compare and Order', gives children experience of comparative language: bigger, smaller, taller, narrower: www.crickweb.co.uk/Early-Years.html

Younger children

Young children need no encouragement to fill and empty boxes and containers. Offer them containers made from different materials, that make a surprising sound when you drop an object in. Model the words 'full up' 'all gone' 'no more' as they play.

Example: Baby Evie loves to play with jugs in the bath (well supervised). She has worked out how to fill a jug up, but is still surprised when she empties it – sometimes over her head!

Footprints in the sand

Mark-making

Mouse has filled up lots of pots with conkers. She wants to remember how full each pot is. Give the children note pads or squared paper and ask them to record this for her.

Cat comes and tips out some of the conkers. How can they record this?

Play a game rolling conkers down a slope and trying to get them into an empty flowerpot. Give the children mark-making equipment and ask them to record how full they have got the pot.

Assessment opportunities

Give children free play with measuring jugs. Let them make their own measuring jugs using yoghurt pots and marker pens.

For a cooking activity, make fruit smoothies or hot chocolate. Ask the children to measure out the liquids and record what they did.

What to look for

Do children use mathematical language in their free play? What words do children use to say which of two containers holds more?

Songs

5 little mice
5 little mice went out to play,
Picking up crumbs to eat on the way.
Along came a pussy cat, sleek and fat: oh-oh!
And 4 little mice came scampering back

(Source: Matterson, E. *This Little Puffin*)

The banana song
Mama, will you buy me a,
will you buy me a,
will you buy me a
Mama, will you buy me a,
will you buy me a banana?

Mama, will you peel the skin...
The skin of my banana?

Mama would you like a bite....
A bite of my banana?

Mama you took too much...
You ate all my banana...

(Source: http://www.educationscotland.gov.uk/
scotlandssongs/primary/mamawillyebuyme.asp)

Additional stories

- The original story is based on the brothers Grimm: the Cat and Mouse in Partnership: http://www.pitt.edu/~dash/grimm002.html

Safety: the conker, the fruit of the horse chestnut tree, is not a nut, so there is no danger to children with allergies: although younger children need to be supervised when playing with them.

Links to other parts of the book

This module fits well with:

✓ Chapter 4: 2D shape and size

✓ Chapter 8: shape, weighing

✓ Chapter 11: estimation and counting out

Number Thirteen – Size

EYFS Maths Objectives

✓ Order two or three items by length or height (Shape, space and measure, 40-60 months).

✓ Begin to use the language of size (Shape, space and measure, 8-20 months).

✓ Explore characteristics of everyday objects and shapes and use mathematical language to describe them (Shape, space and measure, early learning goal).

✓ Recognise big things and small things in meaningful contexts (Shape, space and measure, 8-20 months).

Resources

A set of 7 nesting boxes, and 13 keys, all different sizes and shapes. An imaginary box with an imaginary key.

a nesting set of boxes, they allow children to explore different aspects of size: height and width, as well as length.

Once upon a number: 13

'Lucky' thirteen could be seen as an awkward number for children. It's too big to be counted easily: a prime number, it can't be broken down into equal groups. It's the first of the 'teen' numbers, which are often difficult linguistically for young children: they confuse 13 with 30 and 14 with forty. Thirteen, a contraction of 'three-and-ten' isn't even said as it is written, first the one and then the three. But young children can be encouraged to find teen numbers exciting and memorable, by

The Golden Key

The last story is all about comparing sizes, length and height.

A set of keys, all different shapes and lengths, collected from jumble sales and broken locks, are always inviting. Coupled with

Story outline: The Golden Key

Very tall Hommel and very short Pommel went for a walk in the snow. Pommel looked at the snow on the ground and Hommel looked at the snow on the branches. Suddenly Pommel spotted something shiny on the ground. It was a tiny golden key.

'Where did that come from?' he wondered. He felt around in the snow and found a whole bag of keys. *'If there's a key'*, said Pommel, *'There must be a lock to open'.* Sure enough, Hommel spotted something in the branches. She reached it down with her long arms. It was a big box with a lock.

'This big box must need a long key' said Hommel. They felt around in the bag and found the longest key. It just fitted the lock. Hommel turned the key with a click and opened the lid:

inside the box was… another box. *'I wonder which key will open this box,'* said Pommel. He found a key a little bit shorter. It just fitted the second lock. He turned the key and opened the box and found inside…another box. And inside that box was another box and inside that box was another box and so on until they found a box no bigger than a fingernail. The lock was just the right size for the tiny golden key. It's really little. It's as short as a...

Hommel and Pommel are putting that little golden key in the tiny lock right now. They're turning the key with a very soft click. They're just opening the lid when suddenly... It's the end of the story! So we'll never know what is inside the box! We'll have to put the boxes away and put the keys back in the bag, and we'll just have to wonder.

Story summary

Two friends find a bag of keys and a locked box. They find just the right key to fit the box.

Inside the box, they find another box, and inside that one another, and so on.

Just as they are opening the smallest box, the story ends, so we'll never know what's inside it.

linking them to the idea of a 'teenager', especially if they have a sibling or family member that age.

Why this story?

This story discusses measuring and comparing: length, height, and size and introduces vocabulary for all these aspects of measuring. Children love guessing what's going to come next, stacking and unstacking the boxes, sorting and feeling the interesting shapes of keys. Arranging two sets of objects – boxes and keys – in order of size introduces children to a range of vocabulary about size and measuring: not just 'big' and 'small' but 'taller', 'longer', 'wider', etc.

The uncertain ending encourages children to guess and to wonder, and sends them off to make their own stories and discoveries.

Joining in with the story

At the beginning of the story, talk about 'tall' and 'short': what things can you see if you're tall and what can you see if you are short? When the box appears, spend quite a long time guessing what might be in the first box, unlocking the children's imaginations: *'It's a fairy.'/'It's a jewel.'/'It's a frog jumping about.'/'It's a dragon.'/'It's chocolate.'*

Then mime putting the key in an imaginary lock and pretend to turn it – children can provide the 'clunk click' sound effects!

Once they realise the pattern, they know it is going to be another box each time – in fact one of the things the story teaches is how to look for and use predictable patterns in mathematics. From then on, they can guess what the colour or pattern of the box inside is going to be: *'It's flowery… it's sunshiny… it's pink and heart shaped.'/'This one's orange and pink and blue and green and yellow. It's stripy.'*

At each stage there are opportunities to compare the sizes of the boxes, and to choose the appropriate size of key: a big one for the first box, and then getting gradually smaller. Invite children one at a time to choose the key they think will fit, asking them to explain why they chose a particular key, and let them pretend to turn the key and open the lock.

You can ask the children to describe the key they want, rather than pick it up, to encourage them to use mathematical language: *'the one with the blue top'/'the one with the square bit sticking out'.*

The final box, 'no bigger than a fingernail', is an imaginary one. Ask the children to look at their fingernail and imagine how big the box might be. What key would fit such a box? They have to work hard to think of words for the smallest key in the world: *'a teensy-tiny key'/'a key as big as a baby ant'.*

Finish with the rhyme 'Here is a box' (see page 75), to revisit their ideas about what might be in a mystery box, and to think about things that might fit into the smallest box in the world.

Big questions

- What do you think is in the box? What would you put in a treasure box?

- Can you see a long key? A short key? Two keys the same length? Two keys the same shape? A wide key? A narrow key?

- Will this box need a small key or a big key?

- Which key is the longest? Which key is nearly as long? Which is shortest?

- Why do you think the boxes were locked up? What would you have done with the tiny box?

Example stories from children

Anya hid some keys under the rug. Then she turned a key against the floor.

Anya's story

'I'm opening the floor gate.' She lifted up the rug to find the hidden keys.

There's a key under the floor gate!

There's lots of keys under the floor. That's a funny little one. Now the long one's going in too. (She hid more keys under the rug and then discovered them again.)

Follow-up activities

The sound of keys rattling in a box draws children to it like a magnet. They hardly need activities provided to encourage them to play. The keys get sorted, competed for, piled into boxes, disappear into pockets and the boxes are stacked, built with, filled and emptied. For example, Bruce found a set of keys and spontaneously settled down to sorting them by size. Alice and Ellie both wanted the same key, so they spent a long time looking through the keys to find another one that was exactly the same.

If necessary, set them challenges such as: finding the right size key to open a particular box, the right box for a particular key to fit inside, all the keys of a particular colour or a particular shape.

- **Longer and shorter:** hide some keys in your hand with just the tips showing. Each of the children picks one key: can they work out who's got the longest key? The shorter key? Or use pieces of string, all different lengths, put in a bag with just the ends showing.

- **Bigger and smaller:** have a competition to see who can think of an animal smaller than a mouse or larger than an elephant. What's the smallest (or biggest) animal you can think of? Can you compare a tall giraffe with a long boa constrictor?

- **Treasure hunt game:** challenge children to find a 'treasure' that will fit exactly into one of the boxes. Which box is just the right size for your piece of treasure? Take them all out and see if the children can fit them back into the right boxes.

- **Taller and shorter:** Hommel can see tiny things on the ground: Pommel can reach a box from a tall tree. What's good about being small? Or being tall? Offer a metre rule. Who is taller than a metre rule? How much taller?

Make a height chart and return to it over several months to see how children have grown.

Get a long piece of wallpaper and draw round the tallest adult you can find, to give the children a sense of what 'tall' is like.

- **Heavier and lighter:** using boxes full of treasure from the treasure hunt game above, see if the children can guess which box is the heaviest. They may assume the biggest box will be the heaviest: surprise them by filling the largest box with something very light – a bag of cotton wool or scrunched up paper – and the smallest one with something heavy. Can the children arrange them in order of weight? Test their guesses by putting two of the boxes on a balancing scale and watch how the heavier one goes down.

- **Measuring:** can you find a box that is as long as two keys? Three keys? Try measuring something longer than a box: your arm/a teddy bear/the table. Some children may notice that you get a different answer depending on whether you use short keys or long keys. They may realize that it's really difficult to measure something as long as a carpet with a small object like a key. They may come up with ideas such as using something bigger – footsteps, perhaps, or even a metre rule. It could be a good moment to introduce the idea of standard measures.

Make chains and necklaces with beads or large paper clips, or paper chains out of paper strips. Who can make the longest one? Can you put them together to make one that reaches the length of the table? The whole room?

Allow children free play with rulers and tape measures of different lengths. Measure a child with a piece of string or a strip of paper. Challenge them to find something that is exactly the same height or length as their piece of string.

Circle games

Use one of the rhymes opposite to act out 'tall and small' or 'short and long'. Sing 'The Grand Old Duke of York', marching round in a circle. At the end, stand to attention like soldiers. Can everyone crouch down small? Stand up tall? Or make a pattern round the circle, one person standing tall, the next one small? Then swap?

Daily routines

When you're moving from one place to another, measure the distance. How many steps to the table? The door? The end of the street? Who takes five steps to get to the door? Who takes four? Who can do it in exactly six steps?

Outdoor play

- **Make prints of animal tracks,** cut into large sponges, and print them on the ground to show how long an animal's stride is. A dog's average stride, for instance, is about 0.5 metres long, a horse 1m., and elephant 1.2m. Can the children make steps as big as these? Let them play at making their own animal footsteps.

- **Stand in front of a wall on a sunny day and look at your shadow on the wall:** draw round the shadow (and also your feet to show where you were standing). Come back later in the day. Has the shadow got longer or shorter?

- **Look for tiny things outside:** make a tiny model door and attach it to a tree. Ask the children what they think might be behind the tiny door. What size plates would they eat from? How big would their shoes be? Use these tiny doors to inspire you (www.littlethings.com/fairy-doors).

Using ICT

Simple free apps like Moves www.moves-app.com will turn a phone or a tablet into a pedometer, so children can count how many steps they are taking. 'Millie's Maths House' (millie-s-math-house.software.informer.com/2.0/) includes a game for sorting shoes into small, middle-sized and long, providing opportunities for mathematical talk. Cbeebies has a 'key' song from Furchester Hotel: www.bbc.co.uk/cbeebies/songs/furchester-hotel-phoebes-key-song

Younger children

As young children begin to move, sitting, crawling and walking, their ideas of space and distance grow. Offer them opportunities to stretch up tall, and manageable obstacles to climb, as well as little spaces to curl up in.

Example: On Evie's fridge there is a magnetic notepad, nearly out of her reach. She loves working out how to stretch up and pull it triumphantly down.

This rhyme encourage arms stretching wide:

'Baby shoes, sister's shoes, mummy's shoes, daddy's shoes, GIANT shoes.'

Footprints in the sand

Mark-making

- A collection of keys is an attractive thing to draw. For example, Boris saw some children drawing and asked: *'Can I have a bit of paper? I can draw keys too! There's the long one…This one's the short one…There's a little one'.*

- There's nothing quite like marks made in clay. Help children roll out clay into flat tiles. They can decorate them by pressing keys into the clay. Once the clay tiles have dried, look at the different lengths of the keys. Can they still work out which keys make which marks?

- Show children how to make a straight line along the edge of a ruler. Offer them black pens and white paper, or black paper and chalk, to make ruler pictures full of straight lines.

- Encourage them to make their own rulers, marking off numbers, or if appropriate centimetres, along a strip of paper.

Assessment opportunities

Play the 'which is longer' game. Which is longer – your arm or your leg? Your nose or your finger? Which is taller – your lunchbox or your wellies? Encourage children to suggest different 'Which is longer, taller, or heavier?' challenges.

What to look for

Do children use words like longer, shorter, taller, heavier? How do they approach a challenge of comparing two things? Do they show awareness of size with their gestures and body movements? Do they use any standard measurements like rulers or scales?

Songs

Hommel and Pommel
Hommel and Pommel walk up the hill.
(Two thumbs mime walking upwards)

Hommel's feeling well: Pommel's feeling ill.
(One thumb straight: one bent)

Hommel and Pommel look around to see what they can see.
(Both thumbs move side to side)

Pommel sees a tiny ant: Hommel sees a big tall tree.
(One thumb facing down, one facing up)

Hommel and Pommel spot a place to hide.
They find a cosy cave and go to sleep inside.
(Hands behind the back)

Can you hear them snoring?
(Make a snoring noise)

Let's wake them up now

'Hommel Hommel: there you are!'
(Listeners call out 'Hommel' and one thumb appears)

'Pommel, Pommel: where is he?
(Listeners call 'Pommel'.. Pommel, Pommel')

Only teasing!
(Other thumb finally appears.)

(Source: traditional Dutch story rhyme)

Here is a box
Here is a box – put on the lid
I wonder whatever inside is hid.
Open the lid and let it come out
'Why it's a _____ without any doubt.'

(Source: Matterson, E. *This Little Puffin*)

Links to other parts of the book

This module fits well with:

✓ Chapter 0: hiding the boxes

✓ Chapter 4: 2D shape

✓ Chapter 7: counting stepping stones

✓ Chapter 8: 3D shape

✓ Chapter 12: weighing

Further resources

Section guide

- For outdoor activities: Lee, M. and Yorke, H. (2007) *Maths Outdoors*, Lawrence Educational.
- Pros and cons of children using ICT: BBC website: www.bbc.co.uk/guides/z3tsyrd
- For sound advice about mathematical mark-making opportunities that are open-ended, enjoyable and challenge children's thinking: Worthington, M. and Carruthers, E. (2003) *Children's Mathematics*, Paul Chapman (new edition Sage 2006).

Number Zero

- For an account of a storytelling colleague using this story in an early years setting: McGrath, C. (2014) *Teaching Mathematics through Story: A creative approach for the early years*, Routledge.

Number One

- Vivien Paley paints a compelling picture of the ways children deal with similar dilemmas: Paley, V. (1993) *You Can't Say You Can't Play*, Harvard University Press.
- iPad app 'Cupcake design': https://itunes.apple.com/gb/app/cupcake-design-cake-maker/id538340957?mt=8
- Development Matters: www.foundationyears.org.uk/wp-content/uploads/2012/03/Development-Matters-FINAL-PRINT-AMENDED.pdf
- Early Years Outcomes: www.foundationyears.org.uk/wp-content/uploads/2012/03/Early_Years_Outcomes.pdf
- The cookie jar' song: youtube version with explanation here: http://supersimplelearning.com/songs/original-series/two/who-took-the-cookie/
  Or here: www.mamalisa.com/?t=es&p=133&c=23

Number Two

- The animals went in two by two: www.bbc.co.uk/schoolradio/subjects/mathematics/countingsongs/A-F/animals_two_by_two
  Or songs-with-music.freeservers.com/Noah3.html
- Two little hands: www.nursery-rhymes.co/index.php/home/lyrics/two-little-hands-go-clap-clap-clap
  And bussongs.com/songs/two-little-hands.php
- Mitton, T. and Parker-Rees, G. (2007) *All afloat on Noah's boat*, Orchard Books.
- Spier, P. (2000) *Noah's Ark*, Bantam.
- Sherston Softwares's Mini-matchers: shop.sherston.com
- Revelation Natural Art: www.r-e-m.co.uk/logo/?comp=rna

Number Three

- Matteson, E. (1991) *This Little Puffin*, Puffin.

Number Four

- IMotion from Fingerlab: https://itunes.apple.com/gb/app/imotion/id421365625?mt=8

Other shape stories:

- Carle, E. (1986) The Secret Birthday Message, Puffin.
- Hoban, T. (2007) Black and White, Greenwillow Books.
- Blackstone, S. and Harper, E. (2007) Bear in a Square, Barefoot Books.

Number Five

'This little piggy went to market' is a nursery favourite, but what about this alternative version (for the other foot):

This little piggy got into the barn
This little piggy ate up all the corn
This little piggy said 'I don't feel well'
This little piggy said 'I'll go and tell!'
And this little piggy went 'week-week-week' all over the barn floor.

(Source: Opie, I. and P. (1951) *Oxford Dictionary of Nursery Rhymes*)

- Mitton, T. (2003) *Bumpus Jumpus Dinosaurumpus*, Orchard Books.
- Stickland, H. and P. (2014) *Dinosaur Roar*, Corgi.
- Umansky, K. and Sharratt, N. (2006) *Stomp Chomp Big Roars Here Come the Dinosaurs*, Puffin.

Resources about Dinosaurs:

- Dorling Kindersley, (2012) First Facts Dinosaurs.
- Dinosaur songs: www.kidsparkz.com/preschool singsdinosaurs.html#.VD09cGd0ydl

- Jelly Bean Count app: https://itunes.apple.com/gb/app/jelly-bean-count/id437085790?mt=8

Number Six

- The app Animal Jungle available from: www.sheppardsoftware.com

Number Seven

- Kitamura, S. (2008) *When Sheep cannot Sleep*, Andersen.
- Krebs, L. (2003) *We All Went on Safari: A Counting Journey Through Tanzania*, Barefoot Books.

Number Nine

- Sharratt, N. and Heap, S. (2004) *Red Rockets and Rainbow Jelly*, Puffin.

Further resources

- Albarozo, G. (2014) *The Colour Thief*, Bloomsbury.
- Dr. Seuss (2001) *My many coloured days*, Red Fox.
- Ray, J. (2015) *The Nutcracker*, Orchard Books (a book full of sumptuous patterns).
- Teckentrup, B. (2012) *Spots and Stripes*, Templar.
- Revelation Natural Art: www.r-e-m.co.uk/logo/?comp=rna

Number Ten

- Teckentrup, B. (2014) *The Odd One Out*, Templar.
- Thurlby, P. (2014) *Numbers*, Hodder Children's Books.

Number Twelve

- More conker activities on this website: http://creative starlearning.co.uk/nature-play-learning/conkers-part-1/
- 2draw available from www.2simple.com
- Tizzy's Busy Week from: shop.sherston.com

Stories about filling and emptying:

- Dahl, R. (1981) *George's Marvellous Medicine*, Puffin.
- French, V. (2000) *Oliver's Milkshake*, Hodder Children's Books.
- Gray, K. (2004) *Billy's Bucket*, Red Fox.
- Schubert, I. and D. (1998) *There's a Hole in my Bucket*, Andersen Paperbacks.

Autumn books:

- Potter, B. *Squirrel Nutkin*, Warne.
- Muller, G. (1994) *Autumn*, Floris Books.

Number Thirteen

- The text of the story is available here: www.pitt.edu/~dash/grimm200.html or you can
- Listen to the storyteller Jamie Crawford telling his version of the same story here: www.jamiecrawford.co.uk/listen/listen.html
- Gallagher, B. (2011) *Anansi and Mr. Snake*, Miles Kelly Publishing.
- Hutchins, P. (1997) *Titch*, Red Fox.
- Lobel, A. (1999) *Mouse Tales*, Turtleback Books.

Songs about growing:

The Cherry Tree
One day I found a cherry stone and put it in the ground
And when next day I came to look, a little shoot I found
I watered it, and day by day
It grew into a tree.
I picked the rosy cherries then, and ate them for my tea.

(Source: traditional)

Jack in the box
Jack in the box, small as a mouse,
Deep down inside your little house,
Jack in the box, sleeping so still,
Will you come out? Yes, I will!

(Source: traditional)

Further reading

More ideas for early years maths activities:

- Pound, L. (2006) *Supporting Mathematical Development in the Early Years* (3rd Edition), Open University Press.
- Tucker, K. (2014) *Mathematics Through Play in the Early Years: Activities and Ideas* (3rd edition), Paul Chapman.

Some theory and background to the teaching of mathematics:

- Gelman R. and Gallistel, C.R. (1978) *The child's understanding of number*. Harvard UP.
- Haylock, D. and Cockburn, A. (2013) *Understanding Mathematics for Young Children*, Sage.
- Rowland, T., Turner, F., Thwaites, A. and Huckstep, P. (2008). *Developing Primary Mathematics Teaching: Reflecting on Practice with the Knowledge Quartet*, Sage.

Writing about the ways young children learn mathematics:

- Malaguzzi, L. (1997) *Shoe and Meter* Reggio
- Rich, D., Casanova, D. et al. (2005) *First Hand Experience: What Matters to Children*, Rich Learning Opportunities.

Acknowledgements

My first and biggest 'thank you' goes to the staff and children of Brunswick Nursery School for letting me come and play, for so generously giving me their ideas, their advice and their time. I've enjoyed every moment I've spent with you during the making of this book!

Thanks too to Mabel, James and their family, for the conker games.

Huge thanks to LJ Ireton, for making sense of my words.

Many storytellers have inspired me with their tales and their ways of telling. In particular, thanks to Kathleen van der Weerd for teaching me a Dutch action rhyme I'd never heard before, and to Jamie Crawford, whose telling of 'the Magic Box' has inspired my version.

In my quest to keep early years mathematics enjoyable – and noisy – I've found some outstanding guides. Thanks to Janet Evans, the inspirational teacher in the nursery where I trained, who first introduced me to the work of Zoe Rhydderch Evans on soft play maths; thanks go to Mary Jane Drummond, champion of the child's point of view, who as my tutor challenged me to think about my practice with Big Questions at every turn; and to Ruth Sapsed and Cambridge Curiosity and Imagination, who taught me their inspired ways of child-watching.

Thanks also to Storyteller Mary Medlicott who has reinvented interactive storytelling in the early years. Thank you to Anne Thwaites who set me down the road to learning about the teaching of mathematics, and finding out why I'd been doing what I'd been doing for so many years.

Finally, thanks to my husband Finian for putting up with the noise...

...And a warm hug for baby Evie (and her parents too).